How to ~~Save~~ Survive Your
In-Laws

WARNING:

This guide contains differing opinions. Hundreds of Heads will not always agree. Advice taken in combination may cause unwanted side effects. Use your head when selecting advice.

How to ~~Love~~ Survive Your
In-Laws

ANDREA SYRTASH, SPECIAL EDITOR

Advice From
Hundreds
of Married
Couples
Who Did

HUNDREDS OF HEADS BOOKS, LLC
Atlanta, Georgia

Cover photograph by PictureQuest
Cover and book design by Elizabeth Johnsboen

Library of Congress Cataloging-in-Publication Data
Syrtash, Andrea.
How to survive your in-laws : advice from hundreds of married couples who did / Andrea Syrtash, special editor.
   p. cm.
  ISBN-13: 978-1-933512-01-3
  ISBN-10: 1-933512-01-6
     1. Parents-in-law. 2. Married people—Family relationships. 3. Family. I. Title.
  HQ759.8.S97 2006
  306.87--dc22
                       2006033832

See page 223 for credits and permissions.

HUNDREDS OF HEADS® books are available at special discounts when purchased in bulk for premiums or institutional or educational use. Excerpts and custom editions can be created for specific uses. For more information, please email sales@hundredsofheads.com or write to:

HUNDREDS OF HEADS BOOKS, LLC
#230
2221 Peachtree Road, Suite D
Atlanta, Georgia 30309

ISBN-10:1-933512-01-6
ISBN-13: 978-193351201-3

Printed in U.S.A.
10 9 8 7 6 5 4 3 2 1

CONTENTS

THE HEADS EXPLAINED

With hundreds of tips, stories, and advice in this book, how can you quickly find those golden nuggets of wisdom? Of course, we recommend reading the entire book, but you can also look for these special symbols:

 Remember this significant story or advice.

 This may be something to explore in more detail.

 Watch out! Be careful! (Can we make it any clearer?)

 We are astounded, thrilled, or delighted by this one.

 Here's something to think about.

—*THE EDITOR*
AND HUNDREDS OF HEADS BOOKS

INTRODUCTION

The first time I met my ex-boyfriend's parents during a week's stay in their home, I was convinced that I was cast as the star in a new reality show. The show would have been one of those "Gotcha!" shows where all the cameras were hidden to catch my reaction to most uncomfortable situations. Episodes would have ranged from, "Andrea, the vegetarian, goes hunting and fishing!" to "Watch Andrea get dressed as a 95-pound sister runs around the room crying because she's fat." The Jerry Springer-esque fight between Mom and Dad (over the freshness of a dinner roll) would have been a real ratings winner.

Four days later, I realized the show was my reality. Saying yes to a future with my boyfriend meant saying yes to a lifetime of freshly hunted deer and high-pitched whining. Even though it seemed shallow to cut this guy out of my life only a week later, I believed I was saving my sanity.

Fast-forward eight years: I'm engaged to the most wonderful family: Yes, family. The guy is amazing, but his family was an early selling point that propelled me to agree to tie the knot. This is because I believe that when you get married, you're joining a whole family—for better or worse.

I know some people are happily married to a partner with a less than pleasant family. I wish those people the best of luck. I'm not any less concerned about my friend Lisa, who cries to me weekly about her "monster-in-law," and my friend Josh, who conveniently gets sick each time his in-laws plan a family outing.

Is there anything they could have done differently to keep the peace? Are nightmare in-laws the same with everyone, or is it a chemistry thing? Do things change once you officially join the family? Although I'm happy now, will I be miserable later on?

As a trained life coach, I know how to analyze a person's life and pinpoint those parts that work well and those that don't. But here was a whole new part of my life about to happen, and I didn't know enough about it. Sure, his family seemed great—or was I missing some danger signs? I decided to explore the subject in more depth. You're holding the result in your hands.

If two heads are better than one, as the saying goes, then hundreds of heads are even better. The hundreds of people from all over the country who shared their stories, tips, and advice about their in-laws in this book are helping me, too. You'll read my own thoughts on the subject, as well as my reactions to our contributors' stories, in each chapter. I'm on a mission to get the silliest, scariest, and smartest stories of life with in-laws: I'm determined to get a head start.

ANDREA SYRTASH

First Impressions: Meeting the Folks

There's a Yiddish word—"b'shert"—that means something was meant to be. The first time I entered my future in-law's home, this "meant to be" feeling came over me. I felt the closeness and the love in this family and I wanted to be part of it.

My connection to this new family felt "b'shert" even though it is different, in many ways, from my own. My in-laws live by the principle, "the more the merrier," and have a slight Bohemian edge. Everything is very casual and very warm.

My future sister-in-law's husband also loves this family. He mentions that everything is about a thousand times louder in the house than at his parents' place. My future sister-in-law agreed with him and said that her in-laws "don't yell at the TV like my family does. They don't yell at anything, in fact. But my dad even raises the volume so he can yell back to the hockey announcer, news anchor, or anybody else on television he doesn't agree with."

This raw passion makes me laugh. I find it endlessly amusing to watch my future father-in-law get so excited over the littlest things. He has fabulous energy, enthusiasm, and charisma!

But, of course, my "meant to be" feeling was still one-way only. I wanted my in-laws to feel the same way about me. Did they? I asked Michael if they'd said anything about me. He replied, "Not really."

Many people complain that their in-laws nitpick, criticize, or talk behind their backs. But Michael's parents had not said anything—good or bad—about me! I couldn't believe it. I thought I had made an impression. I thought I had mixed the perfect blend of sweet and engaging; charming and inquisitive. But nobody cared or noticed.

Michael explained that his family is friendly to everyone, but that it takes time to get to know somebody new.

I learned a lesson—relationships take time and first impressions are only that. What matters now is that I feel comfortable and welcome. I do not need to impress or charm. I do not need to do anything. I can just be. What a relief.

My wife's father was a retired major in the Scottish army. She had warned me that her last boyfriend had gotten into a tiff with him, and her dad ended up pushing him down a flight of stairs! I was a bit cautious, but determined not to be intimidated. We had dinner and a brief chat. As I was leaving at the end of the night, I addressed him as "Sir." He shook my hand and said, "You can call me Mr. McMullen." Without thinking, I instantly replied, "Great, you can call me Mr. Allison." Somehow, that broke the ice, and we have gotten along well ever since.

—Gordon Allison
Marietta, Georgia
Years with in-laws: 16

• • • • • • • •

Don't get drunk. I did that the first time I met my mother-in-law. My boyfriend's mom had come in for Thanksgiving. She suggested we open a bottle of wine while we were cooking. We drank a second bottle during dinner. I don't handle wine very well, and I was nervous. We started watching a movie after dinner. Everyone dozed off, but apparently no one slept as hard as I did. I woke up three hours later with grit in my eyes and my hair standing on end. Luckily, his mom thought it was funny.

—M.G.
Belleville, Illinois
Years with In-Laws: 2

I MET MY WIFE'S PARENTS the day they came home from vacation to find me living in their house. My wife and I began dating when I lived in New York City and she lived in Louisville, Kentucky, in an apartment with friends. When I decided to move back there, she suggested that I stay at her parents' house until I found a job and a place to live. It may be hard to believe, but they welcomed me with open arms, and we developed a good relationship. I helped with household chores. I cut the grass and concentrated on pulling my weight so they wouldn't have any issues with me. The only time there was tension between us was when I stayed overnight at their daughter's apartment, and I didn't do that very often.

—JASON
LOUISVILLE, KENTUCKY
YEARS WITH IN-LAWS: 6

· · · · · · · ·

THE BEST DEFENSE IS A GOOD OFFENSE. To prevent hours of family strife and anguish, prep your spouse on what to expect from the in-laws. Review topics that are taboo and will set off your parents' alarms. Point out your parents' quirks and pet peeves. Why stick your hand into boiling water if you know it's boiling? Preparation is your best defense and the key to peace and harmony.

—RODNEY YAP
SANTA MONICA, CALIFORNIA
YEARS WITH IN-LAWS: 2

I DRESSED LIKE I WAS GOING TO CHURCH, and that gave them an excellent impression. My husband had a bad track record with both his parents and his girlfriends, so my in-laws were thrilled with this clean-cut college girl who entered their son's life.

　　—STACI PRIEST
　　PFLUGERVILLE, TEXAS
　　YEARS WITH IN-LAWS: 6

• • • • • • • •

THE FIRST TIME I MET my future mother-in-law was right after Dave and I got engaged. She kept telling me how lucky I was to be marrying her son. I know that Dave is a great man, but come on. She looked Dave in the eye and said, "So, Dave, are you having Carla sign a prenup agreement?" I responded, "No, Gloria, we are not, but if one of us was going to sign one, it would be Dave." I just had to say something.

> Prenup talk is probably not the best way to break the ice.

　　—CARLA HIGGINS
　　OAKLAND, CALIFORNIA
　　YEARS WITH IN-LAWS: 8

• • • • • • • •

THE FIRST TIME MY WIFE, Shira, met my parents, I tried to alleviate pressure by joking around. My mother opened the door, and I said, "Mom, meet Linda. Shira and I broke up." Laughter diffuses otherwise tricky introductions!

　　—MITCH
　　TORONTO, CANADA
　　YEARS WITH IN-LAWS: 2

LOOKING YOUR BEST

GET A HAIRCUT. And even before that, remember to write *haircut* on your calendar.

—CHRIS
WALNUT CREEK, CALIFORNIA

• • • • • • • •

WEAR CLEAN CLOTHES; pressed pants; shined shoes. Parents notice that stuff.

—ANONYMOUS
REDWOOD CITY, CALIFORNIA

• • • • • • • •

I BELIEVE THAT FIRST IMPRESSIONS are lasting ones. So when you first meet the parents of someone you are dating, take the time to look your best. When I was dating my future husband, we had been out jogging the day he wanted to take me to meet them. He suggested we just jog on over there and pop in. But I told him that wild dogs couldn't drag me into their home for the first time when I was sweaty and looking disgusting.

—T. M.
PITTSBURGH, PENNSYLVANIA
YEARS WITH IN-LAWS: 16

GUY TIP: If you're hanging out at your in-laws' house, especially if you're staying there, offer to cook a meal for them. Go out and shop and make a good dinner. This works on a number of levels: It makes you stand out from other guys your wife might have dated, it makes them think of you as a caring and nourishing person who will be good for their daughter, and it encourages conversation, most of which will, you hope, center around you and what a great guy you are for cooking such a great meal.

> Who said food is just the way to a man's heart?

—FRED
WASHINGTON, D.C.
YEARS WITH IN-LAWS: 6

• • • • • • • •

I BROUGHT FLOWERS TO MY MOTHER-IN-LAW the first time I met her. I spent a long time and way too much money picking out just the right ones. But it made the right impression. She told me later that it made her feel like I was OK for her son.

—HANIA
SEATTLE, WASHINGTON
YEARS WITH IN-LAWS: 2

• • • • • • • •

WHEN MEETING YOUR PROSPECTIVE IN-LAWS, don't be surprised at the difference in the home-decorating choices. Shocking pink kitchens were new to me.

—C. C.
SEATTLE, WASHINGTON
YEARS WITH IN-LAWS: 28

BUY A PRESENT, use manners that you normally use at Grandma's house, and give tons of compliments, particularly about the house. I brought his mother a black ceramic Native American pot from New Mexico, where I grew up. Everything in her New England home was so floral and country that it looked out of place, but she said she liked it and put it on display. She definitely appreciated the effort.

—CHRISTIE
ALBUQUERQUE, NEW MEXICO
YEARS WITH IN-LAWS: 3

Dear Michael's parents, I hope you give me the daughter-in-law job!

BEFORE YOU EVER MEET THEM, drop them a note or send them a card. Think of it as the note you are supposed to send an HR person who has just interviewed you for a job. Send a card saying how much you care for their child and how you can't wait to meet them. It's a great ice-breaker.

—CHET YARO
STRUTHERS, OHIO
YEARS WITH IN-LAWS: 9

I BROUGHT MY MOTHER-IN-LAW A PAINTING I had made as a gift for our first meeting. She loved it. If you don't paint, bring her some flowers. Or candy. Bring something.

—MARIO ONCEY
POLAND, OHIO
YEARS WITH IN-LAWS: 19

THE HEAD COUNT

Hundreds of interviews provide us with a rich trove of stories and advice. They also give us a chance to see the big picture through our survey questions. We call it the Head Count; sometimes the results surprise us.

We posed this question, as well as the "father-in-law" version, to hundreds of interviewees: Rate your mother-in-law on a scale of 1-10, with 10 as the best and 1 as the absolute worst of the worst. We assumed, from all the stories and jokes, as well as general monster-in-law lore, that the mother-in-law would score much lower than her opposite number. We were wrong.

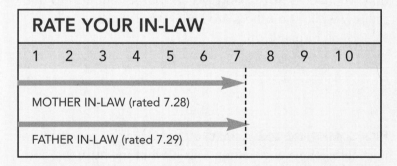

RATE YOUR IN-LAW

1	2	3	4	5	6	7	8	9	10

MOTHER IN-LAW (rated 7.28)

FATHER IN-LAW (rated 7.29)

It's clear, from this highly unscientific poll, that the average mother-in-law is not at all as bad as she's usually portrayed. In fact, pushing toward a highly respectable 7.5, she scores almost an identical rating to the average father-in-law. That's good news.

—THE EDITORS AT HHB

WHEN PARENTS MEET PARENTS

WHEN WE GOT ENGAGED, my husband's parents kept driving by my parents' house. I don't know what they thought they'd see; there's really not that much activity at my parents' home. I guess parents have to get comfortable with the new family they are joining.

> —SHIRA
> TORONTO, CANADA

• • • • • • • • •

STAY AWAY FROM RELIGION AND POLITICS. Everybody's favorite topic is his or her own life. Just hope and pray that whoever is not talking will cooperate enough to nod politely while the others are speaking. If anyone falls asleep, all bets are off.

> —ANDREA WEIGAND
> WOODWORTH, OHIO
> YEARS WITH IN-LAWS: 15

• • • • • • • • •

PICK SOMETHING LIKE A BARBECUE or a holiday to introduce your families to each other. This is what my husband and I did the first time our parents met each other. It worked out well because everyone was well fed and in a good mood!

> —JULIE
> BABYLON, NEW YORK

PREPARE A FEW TOPICS for them to talk about. My fiancé and I made a list that covered topics ranging from Major League Baseball teams to Christmas traditions to family summer vacation spots, in case things stumbled at the dinner table.

—A.R.W.
NEW YORK, NEW YORK
YEARS WITH IN-LAWS: 4

• • • • • • • •

WE HAD EVERYONE, including grandparents, over for an engagement party. We kept it casual and had a cookout. I was on neutral turf at my fiancée's house; it wasn't like one family was entertaining the other. And we started the day by driving into Washington, D.C., for some sight-seeing. The trip helped set the right tone because we had things to do; we didn't just have the families walk in the door and sit down on opposite couches and stare at each other.

—JOE JACKSON
SOUTH RIDING, VIRGINIA

• • • • • • • •

THE FIRST TIME MY HUSBAND'S MOTHER and my mother met, they had a lot in common: They both showed up wearing leopard-print sandals and similar outfits. The sandals definitely broke the ice!

—ANONYMOUS
TORONTO, CANADA

MY MOTHER FIRST MET MY IN-LAWS for Thanksgiving dinner at my in-laws' house. I was nervous about having them meet, and I wanted to make a good impression, so I volunteered to make a dessert. I ended up burning a chocolate-chip cheesecake while I was getting myself ready and waiting for my mother to arrive. My mother wisely baked an apple pie, and she then gave my mother-in-law the pretty cranberry-red baking dish it was made in.

> —CECELIA REEVES
> CHICO, CALIFORNIA
> YEARS WITH IN-LAWS: 11

• • • • • • • •

DON'T PLAN AN ELABORATE dinner party for the first meeting. If there is tension, you are stuck there for hours looking down at your shoes. I had my in-laws meet my parents for a drink after work on a Friday at a little bar halfway between their homes. It was on neutral ground and somewhere neither couple had spent any significant time. They got along fine, but it would have been very easy and painless for one or the other to get up and leave without too much embarrassment if that had been necessary.

> —A.P.
> BOARDMAN, OHIO
> YEARS WITH IN-LAWS: 14

JUST BE SURE TO TELL YOUR DAD to be on his best behavior and to keep all his off-color jokes to himself. My dad had been in the Army and always seemed to be telling the wrong joke to people at the wrong time. But I got him to bite his tongue around my in-laws.

—P.S.
CARNEGIE, PENNSYLVANIA
YEARS WITH IN-LAWS: 25

• • • • • • • •

IF YOU ARE LUCKY, the fathers will have some interest in common. More often than not, it will be sports. My husband started talking about the Cleveland Browns, and both of the fathers immediately found a common bond. It was a different story for the moms, who seemed to be polar opposites. But one out of two ain't bad.

—MARCY NUSSBAUMER
NEW ALBANY, OHIO
YEARS WITH IN-LAWS: 10

• • • • • • • •

MY IN-LAWS AND PARENTS met at our wedding. I had pointed out their similarities before they met each other, and that helped. The two sets of parents got along very well, and they shared stories of growing up in the Great Depression. They had some common ground.

—C.M.S.
DES MOINES, IOWA
YEARS WITH IN-LAWS: 8

MY MOTHER MET MY MOTHER-IN-LAW for the first time at a wedding shower my mom gave for me. My mother-in-law arrived an hour late and breezed into a roomful of women she'd never met before and said: "I'm sorry I'm so late. You have no idea how hard it is to get a driver's license once you've served time." Later, she explained that she had taken her brother (an ex-con) to the DMV to try to get his license. But still, it did not make a good first impression on my mom.

—CHARLOTTE PARKER
DES MOINES, IOWA
YEARS WITH IN-LAWS: 10

• • • • • • • • •

AFTER WE GOT ENGAGED, my parents went out of their way to meet my fiance's mother at her suburban home. Practically the first thing she said was, "Well, I hope he'll be able to take care of her but I doubt it." My parents were shocked.

—N.K.
NEW YORK, NEW YORK
YEARS WITH IN-LAWS: 22

MY WIFE AND I WERE SWIMMING at my parents' lake house when her parents showed up. I climbed out of the lake to meet my father-in-law, wearing my bathing suit, dripping wet. He probably wasn't too impressed with me at that point! All I could say was, "I'll see you after I get some clothes on." It's best to meet your prospective in-laws on your turf, where you feel more confident, and where you know you won't get caught in your bathing suit!

> There's something about putting 'no clothes' and 'in-law' together that makes me uncomfortable.

—GLENN DiNELLA
BIRMINGHAM, ALABAMA
YEARS WITH IN-LAWS: 10

• • • • • • • •

NO MATTER HOW YOUR FIRST MEETING with your in-laws goes, give them a second chance. The first time I met my mother-in-law, we went to her house for dessert on Thanksgiving. The whole family was there. She ignored me all night. When I left, she didn't even say goodbye. The next day, when we met for brunch, her first word to me was, "Goodbye." I looked at her and said, "Excuse me?" She explained, "You left yesterday before I could say goodbye, so I wanted to make up for that." I realized that although she has a gruff exterior, she's actually a teddy bear on the inside.

Consider

—P.O.
NEW BRUNSWICK, NEW JERSEY
YEARS WITH IN-LAWS: 22

I MET MY WIFE IN ALASKA. We worked in the same fish-processing plant, but we worked on opposite sides of the plant, and there was never any reason for anyone to come over to the area where I worked. Her father also worked at the plant; I knew who he was, but he didn't know who I was. One day I was working back in the corner, and he came walking through like he had some reason, like he was actually going somewhere. Obviously, he just wanted to check me out. He didn't even make eye contact with me; he just wanted to get an image of who I was. A day or two later, I was with some friends at a bar, and my wife was also there with her father. We just sat and chatted. I got on his good side because I was doing what he considered "man's work."

—S.H.
ATLANTA, GEORGIA
YEARS WITH IN-LAWS: 10

WATCH YOUR TONGUE

Many Australian aboriginal languages feature a dialect called "mother-in-law speech," which must be used when speaking to opposite-sex relatives-in-law, including cousins. The dialect contains fewer, more generalized words, and is also called "avoidance speech." It is considered taboo to use normal speech with one's in-laws.

I MET MY MOTHER-IN-LAW IN FLORIDA while I was there on a business trip. My husband arranged this when he found out I was going there. We met in St. Augustine, and we were both quite nervous. She whisked me through several churches, a college, and a fort. But then we discovered a shopping area. We both immediately relaxed and proceeded to check out every store and boutique. I knew then we'd be fine. We just had to find a common ground, and it was shopping!

> We both love Michael. Does that count as common ground?

—PAMELA
PHILADELPHIA, PENNSYLVANIA
YEARS WITH IN-LAWS: 14

• • • • • • • •

MY IN-LAWS ARE FROM BULGARIA; they do not speak any English, and I do not speak Bulgarian. When they came to the states, and my husband and I picked them up from the airport, his father immediately started speaking to me in German. I don't speak German, either. I asked my husband why he was talking to me in German instead of his native language, and he said, "Oh, it's the only foreign language my dad can speak, and he thinks any-one can understand it."

—ANONYMOUS
LOS ANGELES, CALIFORNIA
YEARS WITH IN-LAWS: 6

WHEN I FIRST MET HIM, I remember thinking, "Oh my god, my father-in-law is old!" He combed his bright white hair over and sprayed it in a really strange way. My mother-in-law immediately started dropping names the first time we met. It's funny; she's a cleaning lady, and nothing against sanitary engineers, but she holds her chin up like she's really important and high class. I still get a kick out of it.

—SAVANNAH JORDAN
MONTAGUE, MICHIGAN
YEARS WITH IN-LAWS: 13

• • • • • • • • •

I MET MY FUTURE MOTHER-IN-LAW BEFORE I met my future husband. I worked part time in the department store office where she worked as a full-time secretary. My parents had died when I was young, and my aunt and uncle, who raised me, moved away after I graduated high school. I was going to college, living in an apartment, and starving, without food or money. She took me under her wing. She would invite me over for dinner, and talk about her kids. Her son came to work at the store during Christmas, and we started dating. She wasn't really happy with that. She thought he might dump me; he was known as a playboy. She told him that he'd better not hurt me, or she would be coming after him.

—NOLA R. SMITH
TAMPA, FLORIDA
YEARS WITH IN-LAWS: 32

I love happy endings!

IN-LAW FOLLIES #1

I HIT MY FATHER-IN-LAW WITH A FRISBEE the second time I met him. It was one of those *Meet the Parents* kind of weekends. We decided to see them on the way to the beach in Florida. It was awkward when we showed up, and we wanted to take the dog outside, so we all walked out. "Dad" started throwing a Frisbee for the dog, and after a couple of throws, he handed it to me and walked off to water the plants or something. I suck at throwing Frisbees, and my first attempt hit him squarely in the back of the neck as he walked away. I cringed before, during, and just after it hit him, and explained profusely that it was an accident. He pretended to laugh it off. It was a nice metaphor for the whole relationship.

—EVAN
ATLANTA, GEORGIA
YEARS WITH IN-LAWS: 11

THE TWO FAMILIES

There is this weird courting ritual that takes place when two families meet through their children. They dress nicely for each other, strike up interesting conversations, and scope out what a future may be like together. The two sides determine if they want to actively participate and invest in the relationship. Or not. It is a lot like dating at the start. The difference with in-laws is that their kids have set them up with each other and even if it is not a match, they may have to have another date.

The first meeting between my parents and my future in-laws was unplanned. I figured it would be uncomfortable. We were out for dinner with my parents at a Chinese restaurant: Michael's parents, who lived nearby, popped in for a spontaneous hello and a little lo mein.

My parents are slightly more formal (they would have spent time picking out an appropriate restaurant and out-fits), but this meeting gave them no room to plan.

Michael's parents showed up with their smiles and their appetites. They sampled the (half-eaten and lukewarm) Chinese food our family had ordered an hour before, and it was as if we had sat around a dinner table together count-less times. There was something easy about the way they met each other: Nobody had time to be anything but them-selves. It was what it was, and it was great.

MY IN-LAWS LIVED OUT OF TOWN, so the first time I met them, we stayed with them for the weekend. Meeting that way (and for that long) is kind of nerve-wracking. At the time, I was working on my master's program and had no money, so this seemed to be the best option financially. But who cares about money when it comes to comfort? If you're meeting in-laws for the first time, think about a motel or hotel.

—C.M.S.
DES MOINES, IOWA
YEARS WITH IN-LAWS: 8

• • • • • • • •

MY HUSBAND AND I had a whirlwind courtship. We met at a wedding, and soon after I went to his hometown, a small place in southern Indiana. In this place, everyone is married to someone within a 50-mile range. Even though I was from out of town, everyone was very welcoming. His father whispered to me, "You'll be the one he'll marry."

Awww!

—FRANNE DAVIS
CHAMPAIGN, ILLINOIS
YEARS WITH IN-LAWS: 12

• • • • • • • •

WHEN YOU FIRST MEET THE MOM, make jokes. Make sure they are appropriate jokes. If you can keep the mother laughing, you're going to be OK.

—S.H.
ATLANTA, GEORGIA
YEARS WITH IN-LAWS: 10

IF THERE SEEMS TO BE SOMETHING strange going on, don't automatically think it's all about you. The first time I met my husband's parents was at Easter. We decided to surprise them and go to their church service. They were surprised, all right, but I noticed that his mom kept whispering to his dad, and looked totally panicked. I was sure she was talking about me. It turned out that she was concerned because they had reservations at a popular restaurant, and she didn't know if there'd be room for us.

—ANONYMOUS
INDIANAPOLIS, INDIANA
YEARS WITH IN-LAWS: 10

• • • • • • • •

MY HUSBAND HAD BEEN MARRIED BEFORE, and the divorce was a very painful experience, not just for my husband but for his entire family. When I entered the picture, they were very cold and suspicious toward me. I handled this by not taking this personally; they were just reacting to the terrible situation that had occurred. Eventually, they began to accept me. I didn't force it or try to ingratiate myself with them. I just behaved as naturally as I could. Now, they love me. And I love them, too!

Patience is a virtue, I suppose.

—LEIGH DOBSON
TORONTO, CANADA
YEARS WITH IN-LAWS: 25

MEET THE FOCKERS

My first love once invited me to his family's summer home. I packed my favorite movies for us to watch at night, printed out a lovely risotto recipe to make for dinner, and brought my cutest summer outfits.

When I arrived, I was directed to the outhouse in the back and shown where the flashlights were stored. No running water—no electricity—no way! I don't consider myself a princess, but in this case, just call me Paris (especially since I could not stop thinking about staying at a Hilton). My movies, my groceries, and my outfits looked ridiculous.

My ex's father told me to grab a beer and hop in his boat for an early morning of fishing. Beer before noon? Even though this guy's parents were friendly, I could not imagine them hanging out with *my* parents. My boyfriend— a banker in the city—transformed into Mountain Man before my eyes. I imagined that our family portraits would capture me in strappy sandals, my boyfriend sporting his beaver hat, and his father pointing at the catch of the day.

My boyfriend was a catch, too, but if he loved the outhouse lifestyle as much as his father, I had a lot more to discover about how different we were. Perhaps it wasn't fair to judge this guy on his father's cottage, but I do know that you see a whole new side of your intended when you meet his family.

MICHAEL'S FAMILY SPEAKS

According to my father-in-law:
"There was no ice to break the first time we all met and went out for Chinese. I don't see any ice with anybody; but I wasn't sure, because usually people from Europe are very reserved. But your family was a lot more open than I expected and it was a pleasant surprise. Your father is very smart and your mother is lovely. I usually get a good read on people and I knew we'd get along well."

According to my sister-in-law:
"Our families are both very friendly and generous, but I enjoy eating at your parents' house. It's quite a novelty to have a meal served to me that has been sliced or cut and put on a plate. (In my parents' house, you have to dig for food in the middle of the table!) I also like that your parents have white couches and everything is organized. Still, we have a lot more in common than you'd think at first. We're cut from the same cloth—you'll see!"

TAKE COMFORT IN THE FACT that they are probably more anxious about meeting you than you are about meeting them. You are coming into their lives to take away their baby. They know that their child has decided to leave them to spend the rest of his or her life with you instead of with them. They may not even realize those thoughts are there, but they are.

—F.W.
POLAND, OHIO
YEARS WITH IN-LAWS: 40

* * * * * * * *

MY PARTNER WAS SO NERVOUS the first time I met his family, he was sweating. No joke: He took a tranquilizer in the bathroom. The funny thing is, we all went out to dinner and had a great time. There was nothing to worry about! People put too much pressure on themselves. My in-laws later told me that they knew I was "the one" that night.

—E.P.
MILFORD, CONNECTICUT
YEARS WITH IN-LAWS: 5

* * * * * * * *

AT A BIG FAMILY EVENT, you should mingle as much as possible to familiarize yourself with the family. My husband has a distant uncle who works for the IRS. As soon as I found that out, I had him answering all kinds of tax questions for me every year right before I sent the forms in. That man has saved me tons of money, and my husband barely even knew who he was.

—EVELYN RHODES
CAMPBELL, OHIO
YEARS WITH IN-LAWS: 18

I MET MY HUSBAND'S PARENTS during a casual visit to their home on the night of the 2000 presidential election. It was one of the most uncomfortable experiences of my life, in part because I'm a Democrat and they're Republicans. I wanted to make a good first impression, so I kept quiet while my future father-in-law went on about how it was time for a Republican to be elected president. If I could do it again, I would have politely told them my views and that I had voted for Al Gore that very morning.

> *That election would've been a long first meeting!*

—ANONYMOUS
EMMAUS, PENNSYLVANIA
YEARS WITH IN-LAWS: 3

• • • • • • • •

MY IN-LAWS ARE BIKERS. The first time I met them, they showed up wearing black leather. They also had tattoos and big Harley-Davidsons, and they were easily 20 years younger than my own parents. Needless to say, I was surprised. Rather than stand there, quiet and uncomfortable, I showed an immediate interest in their lifestyle by asking questions about their bikes and their trip. This must have worked. Today, we get along great!

—RANDY FREITIK
PEORIA, ILLINOIS
YEARS WITH IN-LAWS: 8

CHAPTER 2

Holy Matrimony! Your Wedding and Your In-Laws

I've imagined my wedding a thousand times. In my mind, I would look across the reception hall and see all the people I love, together in one room. When I fantasized this way, I did not imagine marrying into a family with about 65 cousins. I did not consider that I might not know half the people who will greet me at my wedding. We cut the list down to a modest 300 guests. We are talking strictly kosher (for all the traditional relatives who will join us), and we are talking belly dancers (to represent their Egyptian roots). Somehow I'd always assumed a religious wedding and belly dancers were mutually exclusive!

And then there's the whole subject of kissing. Two kisses per person, is mandatory in this family. I have done the math—I'm going to smack more than a thousand kisses on the cheeks of my guests at the wedding. The double kiss is not just a greeting, it's also a goodbye requirement. (Note to self: Leave plenty of time for my departure.) I've entertained the thought of air kisses, although I think that may offend my very affectionate new family. My logic is that with so many people in from other cities and countries, I imagine that one of the four-kisses-per-person I receive will be infected with a virus that I will not want to catch a few short days before our overseas honeymoon! Will I need to wear a beaded-silk face mask to match my ivory dress?

IF YOU'RE DATING THREE PEOPLE AT ONE TIME, make sure your fiancé is not around when you break the marriage news to your parents. When I told my mom I was getting married, her immediate response was, "That's great! But to which one?"

—CHERI HURD
LITTLETON, COLORADO
YEARS WITH IN-LAWS: 32

• • • • • • • •

I DECIDED THAT I WANTED TO BUY an engagement ring for my fiancé, too. That way, we both got one. I told him he could pick out both rings. My only stipulation was that I wanted the initials of both sets of our parents engraved inside both of the bands; the rings would symbolize where we were going and who we'd be in the future, but we'd also have a little marker of who we were and where we came from.

—SUE GRANT
GREENFORD, OHIO
YEARS WITH IN-LAWS: 9

• • • • • • • •

MY HUSBAND ASKED MY MOTHER for my hand in marriage (my dad is deceased). I think this is something every man should do; it's not even a question. It shows respect to the family. If my husband hadn't asked my mom, she would have been very disappointed.

—K.B.
CHICAGO, ILLINOIS
YEARS WITH IN-LAWS: 1

> Michael asked for my hand and my father said, 'What about the rest of her?'

WHEN WE OFFICIALLY BECAME ENGAGED, I still hadn't met my fiancé's parents, so he called them up to tell them the good news. My future mother-in-law burst into tears. "Are you a good girl?" she asked me over the phone. I politely answered, "Yes." Sometimes, you have to grin and bear it, even if the reaction is not what you expect.

—JOAN K. HITCHENS
CENTENNIAL, COLORADO
YEARS WITH IN-LAWS: 40

• • • • • • • •

IT ALL STARTED WITH THE ENGAGEMENT. In the beginning, everything was hunky-dory. But as soon as the planning started, something new and scary got kicked off.

—ANONYMOUS
TORONTO, CANADA
YEARS WITH IN-LAWS: 3

GETTING OUT OF DODGE

Almost 25% of British couples are choosing to get married abroad, according to a recent study. In the past few years, couples have chosen to wed in South Africa, St Lucia, Mauritius, Las Vegas and Antigua. Although better weather was one incentive, most couples in the study cited irritating and interfering in-laws as their main motivation.

MY MOTHER-IN-LAW and I got into a huge fight over the wedding preparations. She wanted to help, but every time I gave her something to do, she'd do it completely differently than what I'd asked for. So, basically, I took everything out of her hands, and she got upset. I'm not a very subtle person, so there was a series of screaming matches. It would have been much better to set boundaries very early. When you're dating, you sort of let things go, but I'd say stop it as soon as you see signs!

Note to self: Set boundaries early.

—HANNAH
HOUSTON, TEXAS
YEARS WITH IN-LAWS: 11

* * * * * * * *

I HAD TO ASK MY GIRLFRIEND'S PARENTS for permission to marry her. They were ranchers in Kansas. My girlfriend suggested that I go out in the early morning with her father and help him do chores. It was the dead of winter, cold as can be. So I asked him if I could have permission to marry his daughter and he replied, "Son, can you keep her fed?" He was talking about her as if she were one of his cows; it was hysterical. I said, "Yes, I believe I can." He had concerns since I'm a hairdresser. He said, "I only pay $1.50 for a haircut. But if you think you can keep her fed, you better go ask her mother."

—BAKER
ATLANTA, GEORGIA
YEARS WITH IN-LAWS: 10

I'll get writing.

THE DAY AFTER WE RETURNED from my husband's parents' house, where we had announced our engagement, I wrote his parents a letter telling them specifically what I loved about their son and thanking them for the good job they did in raising him. After that letter, I could literally do no wrong in their eyes, and now that I'm about to become a mother-in-law myself, I realize what a genius I was!

—BECKY
MAGNOLIA, ARKANSAS
YEARS WITH IN-LAWS: 28

• • • • • • • • •

MY WIFE AND I DATED ONLY SIX MONTHS before we got engaged. I wanted to get her parents' permission, and I think I caught them by surprise. On the day that I went to ask for their daughter's hand in marriage, I walked in, and the TV was blaring. My father-in-law muted the television and stared at me; it was totally intimidating. I told my father-in-law how much I loved her and how much his daughter meant to me. I was very emotional as I was making this speech—on the verge of tears—until my father-in-law stood up, said, "One second," walked over to the TV, and turned it off. He asked me to start over! I had to say everything over again. Next thing I knew, my father-in-law called my mother-in-law into the room and said, "David has something to tell you."

—D.G.
NEW YORK, NEW YORK
YEARS WITH IN-LAWS: 3

AN INVITATION TO PAY

WE ASKED MY FIANCÉ'S MOTHER to mail our wedding invitations because neither of us had enough time during the workday to wait in line at the post office. My husband specifically told her to have the envelopes weighed, as they would need more than one stamp. When my mother-in-law got to the post office, the line was practically out the door, and she didn't feel like waiting. So she bought stamps out of the machine in the lobby, put one on each invitation, and dropped them in the mailbox. The next day, my heart dropped when I saw half of our invitations sitting in our mailbox, stamped "insufficient postage." It wasn't until the next day that we learned that the other half went out to the rest of our guests with postage-due notices! I was mortified that our guests had to pay to receive our wedding invitations. But we did our best to take it in stride, joking that we might have to give out stamps as wedding favors. Needless to say, we didn't ask my mother-in-law for any more help with the wedding.

—ANONYMOUS
EMMAUS, PENNSYLVANIA
YEARS WITH IN-LAWS: 3

Timing is everything!

SOMETIMES ODD EVENTS give you a clear insight into your in-laws' personality. I wanted to be old-fashioned and ask Melissa's dad for permission to marry her. I made an appointment to see him. He was actually doing my taxes when I walked in. I was nervous, but I finally said, "I really love Melissa, and I want to marry her and would like your OK." He gave it. You could see him doing calculations in his head, and about five minutes later he said, "Are you planning a large wedding?"

—M.J.W.
KIRKLAND, WASHINGTON

• • • • • • • • •

WE WERE FIGHTING LIKE CRAZY over the wedding invitations, because that stuff is *so* important, right? I can't believe tears were shed over it! We had a design for a beautiful invitation that I thought was too expensive. My husband, mother, and I found a cheaper option that I thought was a good compromise. My father-in-law didn't. He called me to lay it on. After a few minutes, he hung up on me, saying it was his money and that was that! Everyone told him to call me and apologize; weeks later, he did. He told me that he'd never had any child speak to him the way I had, to which I responded, "I'm not a child." I think I shocked him again with that statement.

—ANONYMOUS
TORONTO, CANADA
YEARS WITH IN-LAWS: 3

THE THING THAT WAS MOST DISTURBING to me was how involved my mother-in-law wanted to get in every single aspect of planning the wedding, no matter how trivial. When my wife and I were going out to look at the cake, the invitations, the flowers—no matter what it was—she insisted that she come along. And that would have been fine if she would have kept her mouth shut. But she had to put her two cents in on everything. At one point I just told her, "You already had your wedding; now let your daughter have hers."

Boundaries, boundaries, boundaries!

—BEN NOBLE
YOUNGSTOWN, PA
YEARS WITH IN-LAWS: 18

• • • • • • • •

MY BROTHER'S WEDDING was a huge production because of his in-laws. There was a first engagement party and a second engagement party. A first shower and a second one. And two rehearsal dinners, of course. At the rehearsal for the ceremony, a niece was thrown aside by my brother's mother-in-law, who said, "Nobody will see me if you're there! People want to see me!" It was so funny when the niece replied, "Not really. I think they came to see your daughter and your new son-in-law."

Amazing!

—J.S.
TORONTO, CANADA
YEARS WITH IN-LAWS: 4

IN-LAW FOLLIES #2

I WAS LIVING AND WORKING not far from my future in-laws in the months before my wedding. They had an active social circle and generously welcomed me into it, but I had trouble keeping track of every person I met. A couple of my mother-in-law's friends held a bridal shower for me. During the shower, one of her dearest friends struck up a conversation with me, and I must have looked a little confused because she asked, "You do know who I am, don't you?" And, with the confidence that a couple of glasses of wine can supply, I replied, "Of course I know who you are, Mrs. Jones." But she wasn't Mrs. Jones: Mrs. Jones was the not-so-dear wife of their social circle's most dreaded blowhard.

Naturally, everyone within earshot thought this was the most hysterical thing they had ever heard, although I doubt my future mother-in-law found it funny. I attribute my faux pas to the drinking that was a routine part of most social interactions with my in-laws and friends. Pay close attention to new introductions, review names and relationships with your spouse/fiancé before social events, and (most of all) beware of the effects of alcohol on in-law interactions.

—ANONYMOUS
ALLENTOWN, PENNSYLVANIA
YEARS WITH IN-LAWS: 21

MY MOTHER AND I WENT out of our way to include my mother-in-law in practically all the planning. Just remember, you might be on the other side one day, too. So treat your mother-in-law the way you would hope your own son's wife and mother would treat you. It's the golden rule.

> —LORNA MERKEIL
> ELLSWORTH, OHIO
> YEARS WITH IN-LAWS: 9

* * * * * * * *

SOMETIMES, you just have to let your in-laws be more involved than you want. When we got engaged, my husband's mother said we'd have to consult with some of her relatives—my husband's aunts and uncles—to decide when we were going to get married. I said to myself, "I'm not marrying his whole family," but it turns out that's exactly what I was doing.

> —D.M.
> CORTE MADERA, CALIFORNIA
> YEARS WITH IN-LAWS: 7

It would take days to consult all our relatives for an opinion!

* * * * * * * *

WHEN MY HUSBAND and I started to plan our wedding, my mother-in-law not only got involved in every aspect of it, she wanted to take charge of it. When I confronted her, she said, "This is *my* wedding, and when your child gets married, that will be yours!"

> —MICHELLE
> BIRMINGHAM, ALABAMA
> YEARS WITH IN-LAWS: 12

Ouch.

AS MUCH AS IT HURTS TO SAY THIS, don't let your in-laws pay for *anything* with the wedding. If you are able, pay for it all yourself. We let my wife's parents pay for the wedding, as the bride's family usually does. It's not that I'm ungrateful; we wouldn't have been able to do it ourselves. But ever since the big day, I have had to hear over and over how much of a financial burden it was for them.

—BRANDON BUCKLEY
YOUNGSTOWN, PENNSYLVANIA
YEARS WITH IN-LAWS: 16

• • • • • • • •

ANYTIME MY FIANCÉE and I had something serious to do for the wedding, my mother would take my fiancée's mother out to do something else. That way, my fiancée and I could go by ourselves and not feel pressured to do what her mom thought was best.

—ANDREW JESPERSEN
CANFIELD, OHIO
YEARS WITH IN-LAWS: 18

• • • • • • • •

MAKE SURE YOUR FATHER-IN-LAW AGREES to pay for the booze, and that he doesn't go cheap on you while doing it. My wife's dad said he would pay for everything, but then we found out that he had ordered the cheapest beer he could find and bottom-shelf liquor.

—JIM
PITTSBURGH, PENNSYLVANIA
YEARS WITH IN-LAWS: 16

WHEN PLANNING THE WEDDING, set boundaries for your in-laws, but don't verbalize them. Instead, let your actions do the talking. If they start getting pushy or carried away, politely reply, "Oh, but I really want to do this," or "Well, I already have this in mind." This way, you can get them to back off without being rude.

—CANDICE PORTER
OVERLAND PARK, KANSAS
YEARS WITH IN-LAWS: 1

• • • • • • • •

MY HUSBAND IS FROM A COUNTRY-CLUB type of family. I am not. When we were planning our wedding, I assumed that his family needed things to be a certain "Amy Vanderbilt" sort of way. I tried far too much to please them, at the expense of our budget and time. If I knew then what I know now, I would have worked less to please them and more to please my husband and myself.

—JENNY
DENTON, TEXAS
YEARS WITH IN-LAWS: 12

• • • • • • • •

WE HAD BEEN SAVING FOR A WEDDING, but then we eloped. On our first anniversary, we went to Italy for two weeks, using the wedding money. I recommend this. Why use it all in one day when you can spend it over two weeks in Italy?

—ANGELA
WAKE FOREST, NORTH CAROLINA
YEARS WITH IN-LAWS: 8

GETTING PAST THE WEDDING

There is little doubt in my mind that one of the big causes of a broken engagement has to do with disagreements when two families come together to plan the wedding festivities.

My friend's wedding was just called off because her mother and the groom's mother could not decide on the church in which the ceremony would take place. I know another couple that called it off because one side wanted a funk band and the other insisted on jazz. All right, I know the music choice was probably just the note that ended a whole symphony of disagreements; but these times are stressful, and you certainly find out a lot about people (read: your in-laws) during life-cycle events like a wedding. This is a time when emotions run high and money may be low. Here are some tips on how to deal with it all.

- **ASSIGN TASKS EARLY.** This way there won't be too many cooks in the kitchen. Have each member of the immediate family choose one area (invitations, flowers, band, etc.) that they would like to manage for the wedding.

- **IF YOUR IN-LAWS ARE BEING OBSTINATE**, it is better if their offspring (your partner) handles them than having you come off as the whiny, demanding one.

- **YOU AND YOUR PARTNER SHOULD** present a united front to your in-laws. You're the guests of honor and they're more likely to respect that when they see you working together in agreement.

- **DISCUSS MONEY UP FRONT.** Figure out a realistic budget and decide who pays for what. If the bride's family is paying, make sure they're okay with allowing the groom's family to have some influence in planning. Troubleshoot: Work out these details early, before they become problems.

- **STILL CAN'T AGREE?** Schedule a meeting with a non-biased observer—a therapist, a mutual friend—who can help moderate the discussion

- **PICK YOUR BATTLES**—is it really worth it to fight over whether to serve chicken or salmon?

> I'll choose a honeymoon destination far away from family.

WHEN WE FINALLY HAD TIME to go on our honeymoon, it coincided with my husband's parents' vacation, and we had both been planning on going to the family house in Connecticut. My husband's mother had a nervous breakdown halfway through the vacation and ended up in the hospital. Welcome to the family!

—CHRISTINA
CHAPEL HILL, NORTH CAROLINA
YEARS WITH IN-LAWS: 3

. . . .

IF YOUR MOTHER-IN-LAW GETS TOO PUSHY, just tell her to buzz off. Anybody who is pushy enough to tell you what you want for your own wedding has probably been told to take a hike before.

—KURT HELBIG
POLAND, OHIO
YEARS WITH IN-LAWS: 6

. . . .

MY WIFE AND I WENT to her parents' house during the holidays to announce our engagement. Her mother and brother were sitting at the kitchen table eating scrambled eggs. My wife had her hand behind her back and said, "Would you like to see my Christmas gift?" then she stuck out her hand. They both looked at her, and then her mother turned to her brother and said, "Pass the salt."

—ANONYMOUS
SMITHTOWN, NEW YORK
YEARS WITH IN-LAWS: 20

FIANCÉ FINAGLING

I am almost 32 years old. Last night at Michael's uncle's house, I slept in a different room than Michael (my fiancé) because we were not allowed to sleep together.

Not allowed, even though Michael and I currently live together. I've washed his underwear and he has cleaned my dirty dishes. You could say we're used to sharing, and that goes for the bed, too.

But for many in Michael's family's older generation, the customs that they grew up with still apply today. They had to sleep separately when they were dating or engaged, so it is only right for us to do the same. Never mind that they were only 20 years old!

The relationship should be different in this day and age when many of us are marrying later. I am not moving from my parents' house to my new husband's house. I have had many houses in between. I have had many experiences since college. I realize I sound like a bratty teenager when I declare this, but I am not a child anymore!

I want to respect my new extended family. They're kind, and kind of old-fashioned. So I'll look forward to sleeping beside Michael when we are in our own apartment and when we are officially married.

MY STEPMOTHER-IN-LAW WANTED to be very involved in our wedding. She wanted to wear the same colors as the wedding party, which wasn't appropriate since she wasn't part of it. My father-in-law called us on her behalf asking to incorporate her into the ceremony. To appease him, we came up with a bizarre compromise: He walked his wife down the aisle before turning back to walk his son.

—ANONYMOUS
CHICAGO, ILLINOIS
YEARS WITH IN-LAWS: 6

• • • • • • • • •

MY FATHER-IN-LAW PULLED into a gas station to ask for directions to our wedding reception. The interesting thing is, the reception was being held at his country club, where he played golf once a week. And because he was the head of the caravan, we all stopped.

—T.W.
SAN ANTONIO, TEXAS
YEARS WITH IN-LAWS: 33

• • • • • • • • •

The mumps? That's the oldest excuse in the book!

I SHOULD HAVE KNOWN MY MARRIAGE wouldn't work when my wife pulled my daughter, who was the flower girl, from our wedding on that very day. My mother in-law had told her my daughter had the mumps. They just didn't want her in the wedding.

—RUBEN REEVES
CHICAGO, ILLINOIS
YEARS WITH IN-LAWS: 10

Cultural Diversity: Who Says Po-tah-to?

There's a famous scene in the classic Woody Allen movie, Annie Hall, in which Allen sits at his girlfriend's family dinner table, uncomfortable with the stark cultural contrast between her family and his. A split screen shows both families' dinners. His family, energetic Brooklyn Jews who reach across the table for more food and talk over each other all the time, versus the Halls, a proper Anglo-Saxon bunch who sit quietly as they carve the ham. A quick shot of Allen, suddenly wearing the black hat and long beard of an orthodox Jew, tells us that he feels like an outsider—in the extreme—in the Hall household. We laugh because we can identify.

These days, it's not unusual for people of different faiths and backgrounds to find each other and fall in love. But in my case, although Michael and I come from the same faith, we are from completely different cultures. My parents are of eastern European descent, and my fiancé's parents are from the Middle East.

In the years that I have known my in-laws, I learned that hybrid languages do exist. I have learned to ask for certain foods in Arabic, sing songs in French, and tell jokes in English. I have learned that it is OK—and probably even encouraged—to ask a question in English and receive a response in any other tongue. I learned that television should be talked back to (for maximum enjoyment). And guess what? There's no such thing as a car that seats only four. Just when you think one more member of this family cannot possibly be inside the vehicle, a few more climb out. And whenever I think I know who everybody is, there are six or seven more relatives waiting to meet me. Will it happen that I'll absorb their style—buy a 10-passenger van, for example—or stick to my own family's ways?

MY IN-LAWS HAVE A TRADITIONAL Syrian Jewish home. Even though I'm Jewish, I grew up much differently than my wife. One thing that was challenging for my in-laws to understand is that I'm a vegetarian. They were baffled: "This guy doesn't eat meat? He must eat chicken! Veal!" Also, my father-in-law is one of 12 kids. It feels like there are at least 18 nieces and nephews every time I walk in.

> We should double-date with this guy and his in-laws!

—D.G.
NEW YORK, NEW YORK
YEARS WITH IN-LAWS: 3

• • • • • • • •

MY PARENTS ARE IMMIGRANTS to this country, and it's been an adjustment for my husband to be around a different culture. Imagine a man whose family practically came over with the Pilgrims hanging out with a bunch of Indian ladies in saris. But both families are actually quite similar. Our marriage has shown all of us that in the end, values are values, and we are really not that different. Our ethnicities, the fact that we grew up on opposite coasts and in opposite-sized cities, and his parents' inability to digest black pepper versus my parents' affinity for red-hot chilies would make anyone think our families were like oil and water. But our parents couldn't be more alike. They're supportive, they're caring, and they always put their children first.

—M.H.
WEST CHESTER, PENNSYLVANIA
YEARS WITH IN-LAWS: 3

> *I'll order a French/English dictionary.*

MY IN-LAWS ONLY SPEAK SPANISH. When I married my husband, I took Spanish classes and learned the language. I would practice what I learned in class with my in-laws. They were so pleased. It definitely earned me brownie points with them.

—N.E.
HOUSTON, TEXAS
YEARS WITH IN-LAWS: 19

IN-LAWS ON FILM

Whether as supporting characters or holding up the whole story, in-laws are featured in these films. The good news: most are comedies.

Annie Hall (1977)
The Awful Truth (1937)
Best Friends (1982)
The Birdcage (1996)
Easy Money (1983)
Guess Who's Coming to Dinner (1967)
The In-Laws (1979)
Junebug (2005)
Made for Each Other (1939)

Meet the Fockers (2004)
Meet the Parents (2000)
Missing (1982)
Monster-in-Law (2005)
Move Over, Darling (1963)
My Favorite Wife (1940)
Pieces of April (2003)
You'll Like My Mother (1972)

I WAS ON A ROAD TRIP with my wife and in-laws. My father-in-law needed to use a restroom, so we stopped at a strip mall. Not one business would let him use a restroom; they all claimed they didn't have one. Well, my father-in-law decided he was going to show them: he just whipped it out and urinated all over the outside of the last store he was in. Need I say more? I'll be taking a separate car from now on.

—ANONYMOUS
LOS ANGELES, CALIFORNIA
YEARS WITH IN-LAWS: 6

MY PARTNER'S PARENTS WERE IN TOWN one weekend when we first met, and they drove by and picked me up at my house "in the 'hood." They're from rural South Carolina and weren't used to graffiti and transitional neighborhoods. I explained that mine was definitely a mixed neighborhood, but it was fine and affordable and safe, and that I was a normal person. Eight days later, my partner called and said that her mom had seen my house on TV, on an A&E documentary about methamphetamine addicts in the city. They were interviewing some guy on his deck, and they panned down the street until they got to my house, directly behind the interview subject. There's not much you can do about that.

—EVAN
ATLANTA, GEORGIA
YEARS WITH IN-LAWS: 11

Amen.

MY IN-LAWS FEEL VERY SUPERIOR to us because they're sure they have God on their side. They pray for us and make sure we understand that God is speaking to them and has plans for them. They'll say things like, "When are you going to get your child baptized?" and I'll say, "Oh, I don't know. I haven't thought about it." Vagueness is the key in those situations. And if you know there's a topic that gets them going, just avoid it and don't give them any kind of ammunition. You always have to think about what you're going to say and be ready.

—E.H.
MINNEAPOLIS, MINNESOTA
YEARS WITH IN-LAWS: 11

• • • • • • • •

THE FIRST TIME I WENT TO CHURCH with my husband's family was also my first visit to a Pentecostal church. When the parishioners started to dance, scream, and run around the sanctuary, I was in shock! They had an altar call, and people were "slain in the Spirit." It was a far cry from the quiet hymns and choral responses of my traditional Methodist church. The Pentecostal ways grew on me, though, and opened my eyes to different forms of worship.

—SHELLEY
TAMPA, FLORIDA
YEARS WITH IN-LAWS: 22

IN-LAW FOLLIES #3

MY WIFE WAS BORN IN HAVANA, CUBA, and came to Miami when she was eight years old. I had grown up in the north, and the first time I met the rest of her family was when they met me at the Miami airport. It was the middle of summer, and I was dying from the heat. Neither parent speaks much English at all, so when we got in the car, her mother started fanning herself and said, "*Mucho calor!*" I didn't speak much Spanish at the time, but I figured I'd give it a go. It sounded familiar: *Calor.* I thought, *That sounds like calorie. She must be saying that she's really hungry.* And so I said, "You know, I'm kinda hungry, too." My wife and her sister burst out laughing. Then they said things in Spanish. And then her parents burst out laughing. They all laughed for several minutes, until they calmed down enough to tell me that *mucho calor* doesn't mean "I'm very hungry"; it means "I'm very hot." This started off a game that we played for many years. It was very entertaining for the family. It was called, What Did He Think We Said? I never got it into my head that I didn't really know Spanish, and so I would keep on trying to understand them.

—ANONYMOUS
ATLANTA, GEORGIA
YEARS WITH IN-LAWS: 10

MY MOTHER-IN-LAW IS VERY RELIGIOUS; we're not. At one point, I had to tell her to stop sending me Christian-related e-mails, but she respected that.

—SARAH CLARK
NEW YORK, NEW YORK
YEARS WITH IN-LAWS: 2

• • • • • • • •

I DON'T THINK MY IN-LAWS KNEW what to make of my father, since he had been divorced twice, wore his hair in a ponytail, did yoga and was a vegetarian. My in-laws eat lots of red meat and have been married for 30 years, and had pretty rigid ideas of what was masculine and feminine. After he met them, my dad went on a new kick to learn more Spanish so he could have better conversations with my father-in-law. He refers to himself as "Abuelo Julian" when he sends my kids birthday cards.

—CECELIA REEVES
CHICO, CALIFORNIA
YEARS WITH IN-LAWS: 11

• • • • • • • •

THERE'S NOTHING BETTER THAN EMBRACING your in-laws' culture. Never complain about their country. If it's 110 degrees in India, you're sweating, there are mosquitoes everywhere, and your wife's grandmother hands you hot tea, drink the hot tea. Don't complain.

—J. W.
WASHINGTON, D.C.

I'M MARRIED TO A WELSH MAN, and I always considered my husband's parents to be troglodytes: real cave people. Overall, it was hard to relate to them. In the 1960s, I was a proper young woman from Westchester in my Diane von Furstenberg wrap dress and my good jewelry, and one of the first things my in-laws said to me when I visited them was, "The chamber pot is under the bed." Their house was unheated, and the milk would freeze in the kitchen. It was like going backward to Dickensian times.

—SALLY EVANS
NEW YORK, NEW YORK
YEARS WITH IN-LAWS: 36

• • • • • • • • •

MARK GREW UP CATHOLIC, and I grew up Protestant. After he asked me to marry him, we went to his parents' house to tell them the news. We brought champagne and told them we were engaged. They were excited, but about five minutes later, Mark's mom said, "Of course, you'll get married at Sacred Heart." And I answered, "No, we'll get married at University Presbyterian." His mom was heartbroken. She said, "What will we tell our friends?" At the same time our twins were born, one of Mark's brothers-in-law converted to Catholicism. His dad said, "We lost two, but we gained one." They still bring it up. We just ignore it.

Boundaries + Family = Balance

—M.J.W.
KIRKLAND, WASHINGTON

ANOTHER COUNTRY

I HAVE TO ADMIT THAT IN THE BEGINNING, I dreaded going to visit my in-laws. Things were very different than in my family's home. They live modestly, and their habits are different. The towels are scratchy, it's somewhat hot in the house during the summer, the beds are old and uncomfortable, the décor is mostly brown, and they often eat their sandwiches right off the counter, sans plate. And when dinner is served, the pots are put directly on the table with a spoon. I remember that on one of my first visits, several family members just lay down on the floor after eating to take a little nap. I guess that's what you do out in the country!

—ANONYMOUS
DALLAS, TEXAS
YEARS WITH IN-LAWS: 20

• • • • • • • •

WHEN WE GO TO MY IN-LAWS' HOUSE, they are never disagreeable, but they never serve refreshments. We could be there for hours and hours, and they'd never even offer a glass of water. They are not really aware of social graces. So we make sure to eat before going over there.

—ANONYMOUS
SEATTLE, WASHINGTON
YEARS WITH IN-LAWS: 28

MY MOTHER-IN-LAW'S FAMILY CONTINUES to hold on to old-fashioned gender roles; for one, the women in her family don't drive. My mother and sister threw me a baby shower in my small home a couple of years ago. Because they need their men to drive them everywhere, and they live about 45 minutes away, my mother-in-law and her family showed up on the morning of my shower with all three of their husbands and an eight-year-old boy in tow. The men stayed in another room for the entire party, helping themselves to the food. I was embarrassed by their actions, and I thought they were a reflection of me. It didn't help that my husband's grandmother wrapped my present in a garbage bag, and his mother gave me some inappropriate things for the baby, such as my husband's 30-year-old used teether and used, stained baby shirts. But when I talked with my friends after the party, I learned that they didn't think any less of me. In retrospect, I wish I had shrugged it off and took the time to enjoy my friends. But the experience taught me never to mix my friends and my in-laws again.

—ANONYMOUS
EMMAUS, PENNSYLVANIA
YEARS WITH IN-LAWS: 3

IN A LATIN HOUSEHOLD, you have to finish your plate at dinner and ask for seconds. Otherwise, you insult the chef. Luckily, I knew that going in, and my mother-in-law was a good cook. I went to my in-laws' house for dinner the first time I ever met them. We'd been dating about six weeks. It can be disconcerting when you're the new boyfriend and they start speaking in Spanish to their daughter, and you know they are talking about you. Just smile and laugh and keep nodding your head; you can always take your fiancée aside later and ask what they said. I did that after that first dinner, and she said, "My mom likes you because you are so tall."

—ANONYMOUS
GREENWICH, CONNECTICUT
YEARS WITH IN-LAWS: 2

• • • • • • • •

MY WIFE'S FAMILY IS MOSTLY BLACK. I'm white. When I visited her family, I was definitely nervous; I wondered if they'd accept me, and I didn't know whether we'd have anything in common. After dinner, we gathered in the living room. I was on the computer. Someone had shown me how to download music and play it on the PC, so I started playing music I liked. They loved the music and had a great time. It helped break the ice. They still remember that night and the fun they had.

—DREW
SYRACUSE, NEW YORK
YEARS WITH IN-LAWS: 5

I'M VERY DIFFERENT FROM MY IN-LAWS. They are evangelical Christians, and I was raised in a nonreligious home. I don't share their beliefs, but I respect them. I try to talk to my in-laws in their language: For instance, I might say, "That must be what God wants," even though it's not exactly how I feel. But I know that my in-laws will understand that.

Consider

> —LEAH F.
> SUFFERN, NEW YORK
> YEARS WITH IN-LAWS: 9

• • • • • • • •

MY IN-LAWS SPEAK FRENCH; I speak English. They refused to learn or speak a word of English, so I gave in and learned French. I felt that since they were older, I should try to learn their language. Now, they try to speak English with me! We're a much closer family now.

> —L.C.
> PITTSBURGH, PENNSYLVANIA
> YEARS WITH IN-LAWS: 12

• • • • • • • •

MY WIFE HAD WARNED ME THAT her family talked a lot, loudly, and over each other. But still, on my first big dinner with everybody, I couldn't get a word in. It took time and exposure, but I got comfortable enough to speak up and tease everybody about it: "How can you hear each other when you're all talking at the same time?"

> *It is an art to manage loud family gatherings*

> —TONY T.
> SAN FRANCISCO, CALIFORNIA
> YEARS WITH IN-LAWS: 4

WEIRD IN-LAW HOBBIES

MY FATHER-IN-LAW IS FANATICAL about pens, batteries, and rubber bands. Every time we see him, he hands us five or six bundles of stuff. We just say thanks and then sock it all away in a closet because we don't want to hurt his feelings; there must be hundreds of these things in there. We're not sure where he gets the items, but my husband and I used to say that because he's a small man, so close to the ground, he's always picking things up. Maybe it's because he lived through the Depression. One night, my brother-in-law took him to the hospital because he was having severe chest pains—which turned out to be a heart attack. As he was being helped out of the car, he bent over to pick something up. He turned to my brother-in-law, handed him a pen, and said, "You can always use a good one of these."

> —LINDA
> PORT JEFFERSON, NEW YORK
> YEARS WITH IN-LAWS: 30

· · · · · · · · ·

MY MOTHER-IN-LAW'S HOBBY is hiding in her room whenever we come over. In the 12 years I've been with her son, I've seen her fewer than 20 times, and I've been to their home many more times than that.

> —DENISE
> CITRUS HEIGHTS, CALIFORNIA
> YEARS WITH IN-LAWS: 12

MY MOTHER-IN-LAW HAS AN ENTIRE ROOM of cookbooks (when I say entire room, I mean from floor to ceiling, wall to wall, more than 5,000 cookbooks). She also has the strange ability to make cake in any flavor, including Coca-Cola, bubble gum, and even ketchup.

—RACHEL HALPERN
CHEYENNE, WYOMING
YEARS WITH IN-LAWS: 1

• • • • • • • •

MY EX-IN-LAWS' IDEA OF FUN was to get together with my mother-in-law's sister and her sister's husband on a Saturday night, crash wedding receptions, and eat, dance, and drink like they belonged there! They said it was a lot of fun, and there were no other places in town where there was always a live band, food, and drinks.

—S.B.
SOUTH BEND, INDIANA
YEARS WITH IN-LAWS: 5

• • • • • • • •

MY MOTHER-IN-LAW GOES to church every Sunday. She's active in the church, but then she'll take out a pendulum and ask questions of the pendulum. That thing makes decisions for her. I suppose she's spiritual, but it's all pretty freaky to me. In those situations, it's best to smile, nod, and know you're smarter than that.

—SAVANNAH JORDAN
MONTAGUE, MICHIGAN
YEARS WITH IN-LAWS: 13

DIFFERENT FAMILIES HAVE DIFFERENT RITUALS, and it takes time to learn about the rituals of your spouse's parents. My fiancée's family sings and holds hands before the Jewish Sabbath dinner on Friday nights. The first time I participated in this, I found it a little awkward. I ended up holding hands with another guy at the table who was not Jewish, and whom I imagined was also getting used to the hand-holding.

—MICHAEL NOBLE
TORONTO, CANADA
YEARS WITH IN-LAWS: 5

• • • • • • • •

EVEN IF YOUR IN-LAWS' HABITS and traditions are very different than your family's, never denigrate what they hold dear. Think about it the other way: How would you like it if a newcomer came into your family and started mocking all the things you like?

—C.S.
EVANS CITY, PENNSYLVANIA
YEARS WITH IN-LAWS: 19

• • • • • • • •

MY IN-LAWS HAVE A BIG FAMILY (five children in all, three of whom are married) and a small living room. At dinner, my husband's siblings would all fight over who got to sit in the dining chairs in back of the table so they could face the TV while they ate.

—CECELIA REEVES
CHICO, CALIFORNIA
YEARS WITH IN-LAWS: 11

SHOW THAT YOU WANT TO HELP your in-laws. They may not say anything, but they'll notice. My father-in-law is from a small village in the Middle East, and when the family cooks, they cook for the whole town, so there's tons of food. On one occasion, I knew my in-laws needed help with all the food preparation, so instead of asking, I decided to jump in and work. Even though I'm from a different culture and they disapprove of me, they saw that I was trying, and I knew they appreciated the support. This was a turning point in our relationship.

—MICHELLE
TORONTO, CANADA
YEARS WITH IN-LAWS: 3

• • • • • • • •

IF YOU DON'T AGREE ON POLITICS, religion, and parenting with your in-laws, stay away from those topics of conversation. My husband and I live in a totally different world from my in-laws. They are Baptists, we are Episcopalians; they see the world as black and white, we see shades of gray. Discussing these topics only highlights our differences. It is best to emphasize our similarities and not debate issues that we will never agree on.

Perhaps speaking a different language can be a good thing!

—H.N.
OKLAHOMA CITY, OKLAHOMA
YEARS WITH IN-LAWS: 8

NAME THAT COUSIN

Louli, Kookla, Rooki, Dudu, Tito, Foofi, Pompom, JaJa, Sousou and ... Pussy. No, these are not names of my pets or Disney's new cartoon characters. Welcome to my new family.

My future in-laws—Roro and Mimi—were born with much more traditional names, but Michael's family instantly grants a nickname for life to loved ones. When I asked what mine will be, I was told the tradition has ended. I feel left out!

All of these names cause some confusion. It's hard enough to keep track of your new family when you get married, but it's a little harder when each person has two or three names. Wait! Maybe Michael's family is not as big as I think. Each member has so many names, perhaps it seems like there are more of them than there are.

Nah. There are hundreds. My dad has about ten living relatives: Michael's mom has about ten living siblings.

I posed a simple question to Michael's uncle and his four children: "Are you close with your first cousins?" The response—"Do you think we know all our first cousins?"— should not have surprised me. For the next 20 minutes, my future in-laws argued over the family tree: "No, that person *is* related!" or, "She's not dead!" One of Michael's cousins told me that she tried to do the tree until she realized she'd have to sacrifice a lot of trees to complete it.

MY SECOND WIFE WAS A SWEDISH MODEL, and after we got married, we visited her parents in the small town in Sweden where they live. Her father is a policeman, and he didn't take to me; I drive a Harley-Davidson and have tattoos. I had learned a few phrases in Swedish to make a better impression, but when I meant to ask my wife's mother if she was hungry, I instead asked her if she was horny! From that moment on, my wife's dad didn't like me at all.

—BAKER
ATLANTA, GEORGIA
YEARS WITH IN-LAWS: 10

• • • • • • • • •

MY IN-LAWS WERE VERY NICE PEOPLE, but we were very different. They were very conservative and really vocal about it. We spent many Sunday afternoons with them for dinner. I tried not to enter into any political or religious conversations. I would be really quiet and hope that no one would ever ask my opinion on things. Of course, my husband's brother would ask for the token liberal view from me, and I'd try to wiggle out of it. I found that I started to act like them in order to fit in. I'd advise not doing that: You lose your sense of self and can become really insecure. It's fine to hold different beliefs and to quietly hold true to them.

—ANONYMOUS
RALEIGH, NORTH CAROLINA

> *Some people would like an in-law who doesn't know how to make phone calls!*

SOMETIMES YOU HAVE TO CHOOSE between your parents and your spouse, and it doesn't always work out. My mother-in-law had lunch with my husband one day and told him he made the biggest mistake of his life by marrying me. My husband's family is very WASP-y and I'm Irish Italian; he was supposed to marry someone else. But my husband said to his mother that day, "If you won't have anything to do with my wife, I won't have anything to do with you!" We didn't see her for three years, and she lived just six miles away.

—ANONYMOUS
NEW YORK, NEW YORK
YEARS WITH IN-LAWS: 12

. . . .

MY IN-LAWS WERE VERY UNEDUCATED and lived a primitive lifestyle in a small town in Israel. My mother-in-law didn't know how to make phone calls or use a washing machine. Despite this, they were completely accepting of my American attitudes.

—J.
NORTH POTOMAC, MARYLAND

. . . .

SINCE MY IN-LAWS COME FROM BELIZE, when they cook, they cook a feast. And the feast always has to include stew: beef stew, fish stew, chicken stew, oxtail stew. I had to learn to like stew.

—MONICA FRAZIER
CHICAGO, ILLINOIS
YEARS WITH IN-LAWS: 2

WE DON'T DIP IN THIS FAMILY

My friend Jen from San Francisco married a wonderful man whose family is from India. Jen is a touchy-feely California gal who links her arm with yours when you walk down the street with her. Her mother, a hip 60-something, is always the first to hit the dance floor at a party.

Jen's father-in-law is a reserved man who was born during British rule in India. He loves her dearly but would never say it. Jen learned to greet him with a smile and keep her hands in her pockets.

"At my wedding," Jen told me, "my mother was dancing with her good friend, a vivacious gay man, and at one point during the song, he dipped her. Moments later, my father-in-law approached my mother and informed her that dipping was not allowed in public. Who knew?"

All families have conventions that seem less than conventional to the new person joining the group. While dipping may seem benign to Jen and her mother, it is considered an inappropriate display of affection to her more conservative in-laws. Instead of arguing the point, Jen's mom quickly straightened up, but kept on dancing.

The moral of the story? We may dance to the beat of a different drum, but it may be worth taking a few steps to make others (read: your in-laws) comfortable!

DON'T ASSUME THAT YOU'LL FEEL really awkward around relatives whose culture is different than your own; you'll learn a lot of new things and might really enjoy yourself. My in-laws' extended family includes Amish relatives. Their lifestyle is very different from ours. They're very traditional; the women wear the long dresses and everything. Meeting them was kind of a shock, but they were so friendly, I came to love them.

—C. C.
SEATTLE, WASHINGTON
YEARS WITH IN-LAWS: 28

• • • • • • • •

I'M WICCAN, AND MY IN-LAWS are Southern Baptist. There is a line there, but we never discuss it.

—BEV WALTON-PORTER
COLORADO SPRINGS, COLORADO
YEARS WITH IN-LAWS: 16

• • • • • • • •

In my opinion, Jello molds spell danger!

IT TOOK A LONG, LONG TIME FOR ME to get used to my in-laws, who grew up in a different era, in a different part of the country. They served me Jell-O molds made with canned fruit and used phrases like, "Did they Jew you down?"—and I'm Jewish! You must always remember that they are from a different world. If you are smart about it, you can learn to appreciate them for all sorts of reasons.

—SHARI DONNERMEYER
PORTSMOUTH, NEW HAMPSHIRE
YEARS WITH IN-LAWS: 18

For Better or Worse: Being Part of the Family

My father-in-law inherited his late mother's talent for reading the future in the bottom of a coffee cup. Guests at my in-laws' house hurry to finish their delicious Turkish coffee and receive a glimpse of what's in store for them. I bounce between thinking everyone's crazy when this psychic exchange takes place, to desperately wanting to have my turn. In this family, the fact that I'm not a coffee drinker has robbed me of a future. Perhaps I need to take up coffee drinking just so I can join in the discussion.

When my parents first met Michael's father, I insisted that my mom participate in the coffee reading. She took a quick shot of coffee and, when her turn came, handed her empty cup to Michael's father. I sidled over to his chair to hear what he had to say.

My heart sank. He told my mom that she would offend someone soon by yelling at them and making them feel small and insignificant. What? This is not what we lined up for! I protested, but he said, addressing my mother, that it is not what he *thinks*; it is simply what he sees in the future. He has no control over these things.

"Can I take a new cup, one in which I am a nice person?" my mother responded, trying to keep it light. But, in a serious tone, he replied, "You cannot change the future."

My mother is one of the kindest people I know. The prediction sounded so out of character that I wondered if I was witnessing a strange passive-psychic-aggressive argument take place. But if so, how could I settle it? How many people have in-laws who read fortunes?

Since then, I have learned to appreciate the nuggets of wisdom that my father-in-law shares but to take some of his readings with a grain of salt. Whether or not it is psychic or just his imagination, he has a wonderfully creative way to see the world. And I'm sticking to herbal tea.

IN-LAWS ARE VALUABLE, just like the sun. But also like the sun, too close is harmful.

—GARY STONER
MUNCIE, INDIANA
YEARS WITH IN-LAWS: 37

* * * * * * * *

YOUR IN-LAWS SHOULD LIVE FAR, far away—the farther, the better. My wife's parents live in Scotland; mine in Buffalo. It's a huge advantage because no one can drop by unexpectedly. Of course, your phone bill suffers!

—LARRY NETH
HIGHLANDS RANCH, COLORADO
YEARS WITH IN-LAWS: 23

Consider

* * * * * * * *

MY IN-LAWS LIVE RIGHT NEXT DOOR. One thing I have learned is to set boundaries right up front: this is so they know exactly where to cross! My father-in-law called one day to borrow something. I said I would bring it up in about a half hour. I then jumped in the shower. I suppose a half hour was too long, because when I came out of the bathroom in a towel, there stood my father-in-law. He said he came down to pick the item up. I was shocked that anyone would walk into my house unannounced. He just said he wanted it now.

—SHEENA KROCK
KUNKLETOWN, PENNSYLVANIA
YEARS WITH IN-LAWS: 6

LIVING CLOSE TO YOUR IN-LAWS IS HELL. Decisions are ultimately made by at least four people, not two. My mother-in-law knew we were shopping for porch furniture, so she bought us a set that we had to return. I know she was just trying to be helpful; her intentions were good. But there are just too many people involved in the decision-making process.

—ANONYMOUS
CUPERTINO, CALIFORNIA
YEARS WITH IN-LAWS: 3

• • • • • • • •

IT'S NICE TO HAVE SOMEONE close by when emergencies crop up, as they always do. We live about 15 minutes from my wife's parents, and that is far enough so that they can't pop in every day. But it was nice to be able to call my father-in-law last month when I had a flat tire and was stranded on the highway. If we lived across the country from them, I wouldn't be able to do that.

—STEVEN A. PARSONS JR.
FT. ASHBY, WEST VIRGINIA
YEARS WITH IN-LAWS: 1

GROUNDS FOR DIVORCE I

In 2003, an Italian court granted a divorce to a woman on the grounds of excessive meddling by her mother-in-law.

RIGHT AFTER WE HAD OUR FIRST BABY, my mother-in-law moved out of state. I was a little relieved. My wife's family tended to be a handful; they were so crazy and disorganized. I thought it would be better for us if they were more of a visiting family, but my wife ended up feeling really isolated. My family did their best to make her feel a part of us, but it's not the same. Your in-laws may drive you nuts, but hopefully they are a part of your spouse's emotional support, and if they're gone, all of a sudden, it falls on you. Be careful what you wish for.

—J.G.
CHAPEL HILL, NORTH CAROLINA
YEARS WITH IN-LAWS: 11

• • • • • • • •

I ALWAYS TELL THEM, "It's *in*-law, but *out* of my house."

—ANONYMOUS
EAST PALESTINE, OHIO

• • • • • • • •

WHEN YOU'RE FIRST MARRIED, your in-laws should live 24 hours away. After our wedding, my husband and I lived in Texas. My parents were in North Carolina and his were in West Virginia. This was the perfect arrangement because we had plenty of time to bond together as a couple without anybody meddling. Once you get past this newness period, however, it's nice for them to live closer.

—VANESSA HAIRSTON
HIGHLANDS RANCH, COLORADO
YEARS WITH IN-LAWS: 5

ENTERTAINMENT, IN-LAW STYLE

HERE'S A FUN LITTLE GAME my father-in-law and I play: He called me on the first day of April and told me his car was broken down and he needed a ride. I went to the place he told me he was stranded and waited there for an hour in the sweltering heat. He then called my cell phone and shouted, "April Fool!" Every April 1st since then, we make a contest out of seeing who can put something over on the other. I almost always win. You'd think that if you are on the lookout for something it would be hard to get fooled, but you'd be wrong. Last year I had a friend pretending to be a local DJ call up and tell my father-in-law he'd just won $1,000. He's still steaming about that one.

—MELANIE SPLANE
YOUNGSTOWN, OHIO
YEARS WITH IN-LAWS: 5

• • • • • • • •

MY FATHER-IN-LAW LIKES to ride the bus and strike up conversations with strangers. I go along just to keep him from getting arrested.

—R.H.
SEATTLE, WASHINGTON
YEARS WITH IN-LAWS: 20

MY FATHER-IN-LAW WAS THIS BIG, burly guy who always wore plaid flannel shirts. He was an avid hunter and always looked like he was on his way to the woods. One year, I got the family together and said I wanted to have a costume party for Halloween. The catch was that everyone had to dress like Ed, my father-in-law. It was the most fun I've ever had. To see all those people—especially the women—wearing flannel shirts and fake beards was just too much. When he walked in, I was afraid that he was offended, but then he smiled and the whole room erupted in laughter. He was a good sport about it.

—R.D.
KEEZLETOWN, VIRGINIA

• • • • • • • •

MY FATHER-IN-LAW THINKS crossword puzzles are group activities. He assigns clues to people according to their specialties. You'd better know the answer.

—C.F.
BROOKLYN, NEW YORK
YEARS WITH IN-LAWS: 25

Smart!

MY IN-LAWS LIVED A MILE and a half away. We'd see each other three or four times per month, like on birthdays or holidays, but other than that, we respected each other's privacy. We didn't show up unannounced at each others' houses, we didn't borrow each others' tools or equipment, and we didn't offer each other unsolicited advice on marriage, life, kids, or jobs. Given this arrangement, it was wonderful to have them living so close. If my car ever broke down or one of the kids needed a ride home, they were there for us.

—JOHN COOKE
GREELEY, COLORADO
YEARS WITH IN-LAWS: 24

• • • • • • • • •

IF YOU LIVE A LONG DISTANCE from your in-laws, make a point of answering the phone sometimes when they call. When my husband and I were first married, I would always let him answer the phone when I saw their names on the caller ID. I'm a little bit shy, and naturally I'm not as comfortable talking to his parents as my parents. But as a result, I never got to know them. When they would come to town, I would feel as awkward and as shy as ever. Lately, I've been forcing myself to answer the phone when they call. I think I'm becoming more comfortable each time I talk to them.

—ANNE SMALLEY
WOODBURY, NEW JERSEY
YEARS WITH IN-LAWS: 20

WE LIVE FOUR CITY BLOCKS AWAY from my mother-in-law, and although she has no qualms about walking the distance to our house, she simply cannot make the extra three blocks to the bank or the supermarket. She never learned to drive and cannot operate an ATM. At 64 years old, she feels that it is too late to learn such things. So it falls on my husband to bring her on her errands.

—ANONYMOUS
PHILADELPHIA, PENNSYLVANIA
YEARS WITH IN-LAWS: 10

. . . .

LIVE AT LEAST TWO HOURS AWAY from all your in-laws. That's just far enough to easily visit them on holidays. And just the right distance for them to travel for weekend babysitting!

—MEREDITH ENSIGN
FAIRFIELD, CONNECTICUT
YEARS WITH IN-LAWS: 7

. . . .

WE LIVE IN OHIO, and my wife's family lives in Wyoming. One thing I started doing a couple of years ago was create a family newsletter that I try to get everyone involved in. It really helps to bridge the distance. We all contribute, so we are all able to keep up with what everyone else is up to. I highly recommend this.

—RICHARD KAZIMER
NEGLEY, OHIO

SIGNS THAT YOU'VE BEEN ACCEPTED BY YOUR IN-LAWS

MY SISTER-IN-LAW HAS A VERY BUSY LIFE, and I have a very busy life, but a couple of weeks ago she called me and said, "We need to have a girl's lunch. I really need to talk with you." That made me feel so good, even though it's no big deal. It was an hour out of our lives. It was the idea that she wanted to take time to talk with me. It's the little things that really make a difference.

—SHELLEY
DES MOINES, IOWA
YEARS WITH IN-LAWS: 8

• • • • • • • •

MY WIFE'S FAMILY HAS a lot of holiday traditions, and one of the most important to them is the reading of a special prayer right before Christmas dinner. For the first three years I was there, it was always read by my father-in-law. The next year he died. That Christmas, my mother-in-law asked me to do the reading. I knew then that I was a member in good standing.

—CARL PALONE
BOARDMAN, OHIO
YEARS WITH IN-LAWS: 25

MY SISTER-IN-LAW IS AN E-MAIL FREAK. She never calls anyone, but she sends out e-mails like crazy. For the first two years we were married, my husband had to forward her e-mails to me because I wasn't good enough to be on her special "buddy" list. But then one day I started getting all the e-mails, too. For whatever reason, she started to include me in her correspondence, and it was then that I knew she finally considered me part of the family.

—CHARLOTTE KUBALY
POLAND, OHIO
YEARS WITH IN-LAWS: 13

• • • • • • • •

ALL OF THE MEN IN MY WIFE'S FAMILY are the outdoorsy types. They all hunt and fish and hike and climb. I do none of that. When I was first involved with my wife, it didn't really bother me that they didn't invite me to do that stuff. After a while, I thought they should at least ask me, just to be nice. At one point, her brother told me that even though I don't hunt, they all thought it would be nice for me to come along just so we could spend some time together. That's when I knew.

—TIM SCHADE
UNITY, OHIO
YEARS WITH IN-LAWS: 22

THE NICEST THING MY MOTHER-IN-LAW ever did for me was to bake one of her delicious apple pies when I came to visit. It was a small gesture, but it showed me that she liked me and approved of me. I still smile when I think about Mama Queen's apple pie.

—M.S.L.
WAIKOLOA, HAWAII
YEARS WITH IN-LAWS: 37

• • • • • • • •

YOU'VE BEEN ACCEPTED when the phone calls don't always start with you dialing their number. Once they actually go through the trouble of dialing you to see how you are doing, you have been accepted.

—EDNA STENZEL
VIENNA, OHIO
YEARS WITH IN-LAWS: 10

TRY TO TAKE A VACATION with your in-laws whenever possible. That way, you'll get to see all sides of them, morning, noon, and night. Usually we just see a part of their personality when we get together, but being together in a hotel for a week will certainly show you things—good and bad—that you never knew were there. When we took our first trip with my in-laws about five years ago, I found out just how much they love each other. It was something I never really got a glimpse of before. It was really kind of sweet and inspiring.

> *Do we really need to see all sides of them?*

—ERIN DELEONIBUS
PITTSBURGH, PENNSYLVANIA
YEARS WITH IN-LAWS: 9

• • • • • • • •

WE'RE HARLEY RIDERS, so we go on lots of bike trips with our in-laws. We've been to Daytona and Sturgis together. It gets us out and gives us time to talk about something other than work or family obligations. Plus, riding on the open road just feels free.

—BONNIE SMITH
MANCHESTER, MISSOURI
YEARS WITH IN-LAWS: 13

• • • • • • • •

HOW FAR AWAY SHOULD THEY LIVE? I'm voting for another planet!

—RACHEL WALASKY
SEDALIA, COLORADO
YEARS WITH IN-LAWS: 8

EVERY YEAR, I GO CAMPING with my father-in-law, and sleeping arrangements are always interesting. Over the years, we have shared several tents. Not too bad, since we had separate sleeping bags. We have also had to share a double bed several times. One was a foldout couch on the porch of a trailer that belonged to a woman we didn't really know. The mattress was very old and sloped toward the center. We have since agreed that one of us would be in a sleeping bag while sharing a double bed. Also, my father-in-law snores like a chainsaw after drinking. I'm not sure how his wife has dealt with that for 30 years.

—IRVING B. RAMSOWER
TAMPA, FLORIDA
YEARS WITH IN-LAWS: 12

• • • • • • • • •

I THINK CHESS IS A GREAT GAME to play with someone you are trying to impress. And do we ever work hard to impress our in-laws! I was always pretty good at chess. My husband and I used to play against his parents. We would play these little two-on-two tournaments where the players on each team would take turns making a move. But the teammates were not allowed to discuss what they were going to do. I think my in-laws came to respect me as someone who could think a little because of how well I played.

—VAL TOSEKI
CANFIELD, OHIO
YEARS WITH IN-LAWS: 9

HOW TO GET YOUR HUBBY'S DAD TO BE YOUR PAL

NAME ONE OF YOUR KIDS AFTER HIM; there's no way that can fail. And make sure he knows that it was your idea.

—TAMMY NELSON
MIDLOTHIAN, MARYLAND
YEARS WITH IN-LAWS: 12

• • • • • • • • •

THE SAME WAY I GET MY HUSBAND to do what I want: through his stomach. I like to have my father-in-law over for dinner at least once a week, and I always make one of his favorite meals. I know that when he thinks of me, all he pictures in his mind are those meals. And that's OK with me; it's good to have an ally in the home of the in-laws. God knows my mother-in-law ain't on my side.

—JENNIFER MALOE
BARRELVILLE, MARYLAND
YEARS WITH IN-LAWS: 24

• • • • • • • • •

MY FATHER-IN-LAW STILL HAS NO CLUE how to act around me, as I am the first daughter-in-law (he has four sons!). He is totally lost as to what to do and say. It doesn't bother me; in fact, I find it very endearing and funny.

—SIMONE
THORNHILL, CANADA
YEARS WITH IN-LAWS: 3

IF YOU ARE GOING TO VACATION with your in-laws, be sure you schedule a separate vacation with just your spouse afterward to recover from traveling with the whole family. When my husband and I went to Florida to celebrate our wedding anniversary, we were surprised to receive a phone call on the second day of the trip from my husband's family. They informed us that they were just down the street in a hotel and were joining us on vacation. Imagine our shock! They stayed the whole vacation, and the trip was not very romantic or relaxing. My husband and I both found it necessary to take another vacation without his parents the next weekend (and we kept it as our little secret).

> *I'm not telling any-one where we're going.*

—ANONYMOUS
FT. SMITH, ARKANSAS
YEARS WITH IN-LAWS: 4

• • • • • • • •

MY FATHER-IN-LAW AND I are both avid hunters, so we go deer hunting every November. It's something that we both look forward to. Even though we don't always see eye to eye, we always have that time together to work things out and talk. I think you have to try to find something you have in common.

—J.J.
BULGER, PENNSYLVANIA
YEARS WITH IN-LAWS: 3

MY SPOUSE'S EXTENDED FAMILY and my family (we each have two married siblings) took a cruise to Alaska together. I was skeptical at first, but the trip went surprisingly well. We hiked and explored on day trips, and I was able to see my new family as active, happy people. My father-in-law wants to go camping with us. My mother-in-law thinks they'll probably just stay in a cabin in the park, but I hope my father-in-law and husband will go into the backcountry for a night or two. My husband loves nature; for him to see a bear with my father-in-law would be a great experience for them to share.

—D.M.
BERKELEY, CALIFORNIA
YEARS WITH IN-LAWS: 3

• • • • • • • •

MY IN-LAWS TREAT MY HUSBAND like he is still part of their family, as if the kids and I don't exist. This past Father's Day, my dad invited us over for a barbeque and swimming. The plan was that my husband would visit his dad for a few hours and then meet me and the kids at my dad's house. Five hours later, my husband called me at my dad's house to tell me that he wouldn't be able to make it because he was still with his dad.

—DENISE
CITRUS HEIGHTS, CALIFORNIA
YEARS WITH IN-LAWS: 12

HOW TO GET YOUR WIFE'S MOM TO BE YOUR PAL

BECOME A GOOD LISTENER. Ask her about her job or her kids or her bridge party. Whatever is important to her, ask about it often and really listen to her responses. If she gets the idea that you care about her and the things that are important to her, she'll like you. I'd always start any conversation with my mother-in-law by asking what was new and exciting in her life. She always had something to tell me, and I always listened.

—DONALD WINKLE
ELLSWORTH, OHIO
YEARS WITH IN-LAWS: 6

• • • • • • • •

I SUGGESTED THAT MY MOTHER-IN-LAW and I shop for a birthday present for my wife. It was a fun afternoon together—the first time I had ever spent time alone with her. I know she felt useful and needed, but we both knew it wasn't about me deferring to her taste or prediction of what her daughter might want for a gift. It was about a nice, unfettered interaction between a son-in-law and his mother-in-law.

—ANONYMOUS
CLEVELAND, OHIO
YEARS WITH IN-LAWS: 1

IF YOU WANT TO PLAN A VACATION in secret and surprise your wife with it, use your mother-in-law as your secret helper. Tell her what you're doing and ask her for suggestions. Let her help in the surprise part. She'll get a kick out of it, and she'll also realize what a great guy you are for doing such a thing.

—ALLAN
ATLANTA, GEORGIA
YEARS WITH IN-LAWS: 10

• • • • • • • •

FIGURE OUT SOMETHING YOU SHARE an interest in. It can be anything—politics, flowers, baseball—as long as you both enjoy talking about it. For my mother-in-law and me, this topic is broadcasting. She used to own two radio stations, and I worked for many years at CNN, so if things get boring or tense, I can say something as simple as, "What do you think about the new president of NBC?" Suddenly, a civil, interesting conversation ensues.

—DAVID BERNKNOPF
ATLANTA, GEORGIA
YEARS WITH IN-LAWS: 13

I **BONDED WITH MY MOTHER-IN-LAW** over crafts. She was a quilter, and I was a knitter, but I let her teach me how to quilt. Those hours we spent together were really nice, without all the pressure of a family gathering, and it allowed us to get to know one another.

—GRACE
CHAPEL HILL, NORTH CAROLINA
YEARS WITH IN-LAWS: 22

• • • • • • • •

MY MOTHER-IN-LAW IS AS BIG a Broncos and Rockies fan as I am. Early on, I got in good by going to games with her—and being one of the few people who actually stayed until the end instead of leaving early to beat the traffic.

—ROB MCHARGUE
SAN ANTONIO, TEXAS
YEARS WITH IN-LAWS: 18

• • • • • • • •

I **FOUND OUT WHAT MY IN-LAWS** and I had in common: My mother-in-law and I both love arts and crafts, and my father-in-law and I both love to read. I make sure to e-mail them occasionally or say something during a phone call about reading recommendations or do-it-yourself projects.

—ANNE B.
SAN FRANCISCO, CALIFORNIA
YEARS WITH IN-LAWS: 2

AS AN ADULT, THE MOST FUN GAMES to play are the ones that were intended for children. You will never laugh harder or have more fun than by playing something like Chutes and Ladders or Candy Land with adults, including your in-laws. It's so much fun because of the juvenile nature of the game. I used to laugh every time my mother-in-law landed on a chute and had to go way back down to the bottom of the board. Usually she wasn't laughing.

—L.H.
BAZETTA, OHIO
YEARS WITH IN-LAWS: 24

• • • • • • • •

DON'T HELP YOUR FATHER-IN-LAW with mechanical things or carpentry if you don't know what you're doing, because it only makes things worse. Instead of proving you're an idiot, just let him assume it.

—JOHN COOKE
GREELEY, COLORADO
YEARS WITH IN-LAWS: 24

• • • • • • • •

MY FATHER-IN-LAW WILL INVITE ME out for lunch and suggest that I drive. Or he'll say, "Let's go fishing—you figure out the details, and I'll just come along." In return, I make an effort to communicate with him about crucial life events.

—DOUG BRIMMER
COLORADO SPRINGS, COLORADO
YEARS WITH IN-LAWS: 13

SPECIAL CONSIDERATION: THE MAMA'S BOY

MY MOTHER-IN-LAW SEES ME just as someone who bore her two grandchildren. But my husband is like *her* husband; he's the guy in her life.

—ANONYMOUS
CHICAGO, ILLINOIS
YEARS WITH IN-LAWS: 6

• • • • • • • • •

THERE MAY NOT BE A SOLUTION to the mama's-boy syndrome. The real issue seems to be the total flexibility of the son's backbone, an amazing medical phenomenon. When said son is confronted with a decision that even remotely pressures him into choosing a path away from Mom, he falters. Your strong, level-headed, and loving mate turns five years old and gets scared of making Mommy mad. It's very real and very frightening. When faced with a mama's boy outbreak, practical tonics include deep breathing (four counts in and four counts out), Bikram yoga, a 12-mile run, shiatsu massage, a manicure/pedicure combo, or a quick chapter read of either *The Onion*'s latest book for comic relief or *Boundaries in Marriage* by Dr. Henry Cloud and Dr. John Townsend.

—J.P.
SEATTLE, WASHINGTON
YEARS WITH IN-LAWS: 6

MY HUSBAND IS A PERFECT SPECIMEN of a mama's boy. He looked to his mother to take care of everything, ranging from his laundry to where to attend college. She would visit him whenever she wanted, make his dinner, clean his apartment, do his shopping, or whatever she felt needed to be done. After we were married, she thought this behavior would continue. I quickly made it clear to my husband and mother-in-law that she would have to follow a new set of rules: mine. It was difficult, but it's working out well. I still let her iron his shirts, though.

—WENDY
MIAMI, FLORIDA
YEARS WITH IN-LAWS: 7

• • • • • • • • •

MY HUSBAND WOULD FOLLOW BEHIND me and redo chores I had done around the house. He'd refold the towels the way his mother did, or take everything out of the dishwasher and reload it the way his mother did. So I went on strike and wouldn't do his laundry or the dishes: if he was going to redo what I had already done, then he could do it his way and I wouldn't bother. After about two weeks of dishes piling up in the sink and going without clean socks, he finally relented and promised to let me do things my way. It bothered me to no end to have a sink full of dirty dishes, but I was not giving in.

—SHELLEY BEAUMONT
GRANDVIEW, TEXAS
YEARS WITH IN-LAWS: 4

I WENT ON VACATION WITH my husband's entire family. On our flight home, our seats on the plane were not with his family. The next day, my mother-in-law called to scream at me for not sitting next to my sister-in-law on the plane. She told me that because I didn't try to switch the seats, I was not family oriented. My husband did not stand up for me. We eventually went to therapy, but he couldn't see how unnatural and messed up his behavior was. The therapist helped me see that at age 39, there was a slim chance that this behavior would ever change. We broke up in the end.

—ANONYMOUS
LOS ANGELES, CALIFORNIA
YEARS WITH IN-LAWS: 1

• • • • • • • •

MY HUSBAND TREATS HIS MOTHER BADLY. He doesn't return her phone calls, he talks to her abruptly, he doesn't listen when she talks, and he never asks how she is doing. It is sad, really. I try to make up for my husband's behavior by treating her like I treat perfect strangers: with common decency. I ask her how she is doing and help out when I can. Most of the time, she just needs someone to listen to her. And I listen patiently, even though it may be the fifth time I have heard about her vacation. Most of the time, she is grateful to know that she now has a method of communicating to her son: me.

—DONNA
ALAMEDA, CALIFORNIA
YEARS WITH IN-LAWS: 3

ALWAYS REMEMBER THAT your mother-in-law is your husband's mother. You may be fortunate to consider her a friend, too, but no matter how tempting it is to unload on her about him, don't do it. In the beginning of my marriage, my husband and I had some problems. When my mother-in-law called, I'd sometimes complain about my husband to her. That is not good. It created a distance between us for a while, because I think she would rather not have heard it. I caught myself, remembering that he is her son. I realized that she feels toward him as I will feel toward my own kids. Even if a mother knows in her heart of hearts that her child is a brat, she doesn't want to hear that from someone else.

—ANONYMOUS
READING, PENNSYLVANIA
YEARS WITH IN-LAWS: 4

. . . .

MY FAVORITE THING TO DO with my in-laws is go to museums. It's much better than fielding my mother-in-law's questions about when we're going to start having children. It's safer to keep the coversation to some other woman's plight—like Frida Kahlo's!

—L.
SAN FRANCISCO, CALIFORNIA

IN-LAWS AND COMPETITIVE GAMES

IF WE'RE PLAYING A FAMILY GAME, I don't let my in-laws win. They get no special treatment from me. I try to beat them, just like I try to beat everyone else. Our game is gin rummy, and I love rubbing it in their faces. And it lets them know that you can't be pushed around in other facets of your relationship with them.

—CHAD MORTON
POLAND, OHIO
YEARS WITH IN-LAWS: 21

• • • • • • • •

GET A SENSE OF WHAT SPORTS team your father-in-law likes. It's best not to bash his alma mater or favorite pro team.

—ANONYMOUS
OAKLAND, CALIFORNIA

• • • • • • • •

WE WERE PLAYING CHARADES one night. I drew the movie title *Deep Throat*. I don't think my mother-in-law ever looked at me the same way again after I had to act that out!

—SHELLEY BEAUMONT
GRANDVIEW, TEXAS
YEARS WITH IN-LAWS: 4

JUST MAKE SURE YOU WIN, whatever it takes.

—J.P.
SEATTLE, WASHINGTON
YEARS WITH IN-LAWS: 6

• • • • • • • •

WHEN MY FAMILY GETS TOGETHER and plays games, it generally turns into a trash-talking, uncomfortably serious competition during which, at some point, one side accuses the other side of cheating. But it's not like that with my wife's family. We usually play Yahtzee or cards, and my wife's mother is very good and very lucky, like me. But instead of seeing her as competition, I make sure it's known that I am on her side. I cheer for her when she rolls Yahtzee, and I try to get my hands on the die as soon as possible to "capture" some of her talent or luck. This works; we get along great in these moments. And the games are inevitably more enjoyable than the knock-down competitions with my own family. Although, when you win in my family, you've really earned it.

—ANONYMOUS
TAMPA, FLORIDA
YEARS WITH IN-LAWS: 10

ONCE WE HELPED MY MOTHER-IN-LAW MOVE, only to find that she had packed everything from the last 20 years of living in the same place. We were tired and hot, and when we saw she had packed spices that were at least 10 years old, we'd had enough. We started throwing whole boxes in the trash—without asking—so we didn't have to move them. She was so mad at us when she found out. We still laugh over it. Sometimes you have to join forces to survive.

—ANONYMOUS
ATLANTA, GEORGIA
YEARS WITH IN-LAWS: 10

* * * * * * * *

I WAS 17 WHEN I GOT MARRIED. Because I was so young, my in-laws tried to mold me into what they wanted me to be. They complained if I didn't send birthday cards, make coffee in the morning, invite certain people over to my house . . . the list goes on and on. I wasn't mature enough to stand up to them. For about 10 years, I neglected my own family and spent most holidays with theirs. Finally, my husband and I decided to move out of state to get away from them, and things got much better. My advice to the young brides out there: Be careful! You're especially vulnerable to "in-law shaping" when you get married so young. If you know this before walking down the aisle, however, it will be a lot easier to deal with.

> *I hope I'm okay at my age.*

—JANIS HACKETT
CENTENNIAL, COLORADO
YEARS WITH IN-LAWS: 38

MY FATHER-IN-LAW IS A CRASS, vulgar man with no boundaries. When we did anything that involved him, we would tell people to expect the worst so they wouldn't be completely knocked completely off guard. With someone like him, all you can do is warn people.

> —LINDA
> PORT JEFFERSON, NEW YORK
> YEARS WITH IN-LAWS: 30

• • • • • • • •

I LOVE TO SKI WITH MY IN-LAWS, who are in their early 70s. They're a bit more cautious now, and I guess we can't always count on them being physically able. But it's truly a wonderful day to spend with them. My mother-in-law is cute: She'll take a hot chocolate break every few runs.

> —ANONYMOUS
> ORINDA, CALIFORNIA

• • • • • • • •

AFTER WE MOVED FROM NEW ENGLAND to Alabama, my wife's mother was acting like the umbilical cord was still attached. She was telling my wife how horrible I was for taking her daughter away. My wife told me how horrible her mother was making her feel. I told her, "You're 29 years old. It's either me or your mother, because I have to be down here." And after that she chose me, luckily.

I hate ultimatums!

> —ANONYMOUS
> BIRMINGHAM, ALABAMA
> YEARS WITH IN-LAWS: 4

ENTER THE IN-LAWS

With new in-laws, you suddenly have authority figures telling you how to live and what to do. It is strange enough to have Mom and Dad doing that when you are an adult but you are used to your parents' ways. You have adapted to them and perfected your arguments with them. Years of living together (especially during your teen years) have pushed you and your immediate family to the limit. You know who they are and how they operate. Enter the in-laws.

You think, "Who are you? I've known my favorite TV families longer than I've known you. Why are you telling me what I should do, say, or buy?!"

They are telling you because you are the one who married their precious child and you have to take care of him or her. They are telling you because you may bear their grandchildren, and you may even care for them when they are old! And, they are probably telling you because deep down, they love to tell other people what to do.

WHEN BOTH OF US WERE IN THE ROOM, my husband's mother would only talk to him. So to get her to include me in the conversation, I would sit literally between them so she would have to look past me to talk to him. And I would add a few words every now and then. I think that was a good strategy.

—JEANIE CLINTON
NEW ORLEANS, LOUISIANA
YEARS WITH IN-LAWS: 20

Sounds cozy—and totally uncomfortable.

• • • • • • • •

MY HUSBAND HAS TO SPEAK to his father on the phone every single day. The only thing they ever talk about is sports. If something is happening in sports, I can assure you that they are covering it. My big problem with this was my obscenely expensive phone bills. The good news is that we switched to an Internet phone service, and now our long-distance calls are free.

—ANONYMOUS
LOS ANGELES, CALIFORNIA
YEARS WITH IN-LAWS: 6

But doesn't that also mean more calls?

• • • • • • • •

ALWAYS BE COMPLIMENTARY and build up your husband in front of his parents. Ultimately, their biggest concern is his happiness, and if they feel that he's content, things between you and your in-laws are going to be great.

—FRANS WILLS
LITTLETON, COLORADO
YEARS WITH IN-LAWS: 5

> Freud would have nothing major to write about with my mother-in-law.

I'M CONVINCED THAT BECAUSE she never remarried, my mother-in-law looks at my husband as her man. When she was in town visiting, I got the feeling she didn't want me there with her and him. We'd be watching TV and I would have my hand on his leg, and she would reach over and put her hand on his other leg. It was totally creepy! My husband has since told her not to do those things. He came to that realization on his own, and I think that was important. I wanted my husband to set his own boundaries. I didn't want to be the person changing his relationship with his mom.

—ANONYMOUS
CHICAGO, ILLINOIS
YEARS WITH IN-LAWS: 6

* * * * * * * *

I LOVE BOTH MY WIFE AND MY MOTHER very much, but there seems to be some tension. It's as if my wife needs an archenemy and has decided it will be my mom. After a great dinner, my wife will say something like, "Did you hear when your mom said this or that?" She always wants to find the worst things, and I tell her to leave me out of the complaining, that it's "between you and my mom." In public, you always have to take your wife's side because you *live* with your wife. That doesn't mean in your heart you have to believe it, but when you're sitting between them, it's better to side with the woman you go home with.

—D.G.
NEW YORK, NEW YORK
YEARS WITH IN-LAWS: 3

IT MAY NOT SEEM FAIR THAT YOU are the one running through the mall to buy her Mother's Day gift and her birthday gift, or that you have to sit and smile when she gives criticism while your husband blindly looks on. But in the end, you'll feel better for always doing the right thing—even if she doesn't appreciate it.

—JENNIFER
DALLAS, TEXAS
YEARS WITH IN-LAWS: 4

• • • • • • • •

MY IN-LAWS HATE ME—well, most of them. I was never given a chance. I was the guy that came between, during, and after the longtime (junior high) boyfriend my mother-in-law so adored. You know, the one that "grew up" with the family; a regular at family gatherings and vacations; his school pictures strategically placed everywhere; a Christmas stocking with his name in glitter-glue. My mother-in-law is the source of the hate. Her husband, my wife's stepfather, therefore hates me too. I knew I was doomed the first time I came to pick up my wife and her mother turned her back on me as she slammed the door in my face. The good news, though, is that I'm never expected to go to Sunday dinner.

—K.
ATLANTA, GEORGIA
YEARS WITH IN-LAWS: 6

MY BEST MEMORY OF MY IN-LAWS was watching my father-in-law pour water down a gopher hole and seeing the gophers come out of another hole soaking wet. We all laughed hysterically.

—ANONYMOUS
OAK LAWN, ILLINOIS
YEARS WITH IN-LAWS: 36

• • • • • • • • •

I REALLY THINK MY WIFE IS NOT BIOLOGICALLY related to her parents; she's so different from them. I tell her that I think they found her on the side of the road when she was a baby. A few summers ago, I took them to San Diego for two nights. Their room cost me about $500 a night, and all they did was complain about it. They never even thanked me for the vacation. They didn't even buy us dinner.

—ANONYMOUS
LOS ANGELES, CALIFORNIA
YEARS WITH IN-LAWS: 6

5

Getting Together: Visiting, Pro and Con

Many of our respondents—and many people I know—complain about how overbearing their in-laws are, "They just walk in, start fixing things, cleaning up and putting food in my fridge!"

Um. What's the issue again?

When we moved into our 450-square-foot, "deluxe hallway" apartment in Manhattan, on one of the hottest days of the summer, my in-laws immediately started to clean up and re-organize our place, just as my parents would have done. My mother-in-law cleaned out the refrigerator as I hauled boxes up our five flights of stairs, and my father-in-law ran to the hardware store to purchase a new air-conditioning unit for our bedroom window.

Not only was my fridge sparkling, it was full of middle-eastern foods—olives, pita, zatar spice, a way too salty cheese, and this strange, stale, sesame biscuit that is supposed to be a delicious snack.

I want to publicly declare that my in-laws are welcome, and even encouraged, to help me with my housework any time. They are invited to place food in my refrigerator. They will not disrupt the artistic way I leave some items spread out at home. They are free to add their own flair.

If your in-laws are cleaning up your home, you can choose to see that as a burden or you can choose to see that as a blessing. Of course, it's another story if they are rearranging your furniture and completely ruining your feng shui. But if it's just a dust bunny here or there, or some new dish to enjoy (or toss out after they've gone), is it really so bad?

ACCEPT THAT YOUR IN-LAWS won't always say "thank you" when you make extra efforts for them. When my in-laws came to visit us, we paid for their trip. But we also paid for them to go to Spain, stay in four-star hotels, and rent a convertible. All they did was complain about the weather, the food, and the room. But we were happy to do it because it helps to maintain the relationship. We drew the line, though, when they wanted us to give them spending money!

—M.S.
TORONTO, CANADA
YEARS WITH IN-LAWS: 18

• • • • • • • •

FRIDAY NIGHT IS A GOOD NIGHT to clean house, so if your in-laws show up unannounced on Saturday morning for breakfast, at least your home won't be a pigsty.

—CECELIA REEVES
CHICO, CALIFORNIA
YEARS WITH IN-LAWS: 11

Show up unannounced? Eek!

• • • • • • • •

YOU SHOULD NOT DRINK. Who knows what might come out of your mouth once you have a few drinks in you? You might actually tell them what you think of them; instead, play it safe and drink your Coke without the rum.

—PATRICK CALIENDO
POLAND, OHIO
YEARS WITH IN-LAWS: 26

Very true!

YOUR SPOUSE WILL GENERALLY be more stressed by his or her parents visiting than you will be. I find it's best to plan some activities to get out of the house; everyone has a good time and relaxes. And the more relaxed your spouse is, the happier you'll be.

——ANONYMOUS
SAN JOSE, CALIFORNIA

• • • • • • • •

THE GREATEST INVENTION FOR DEALING with family get-togethers is the Game Boy. It's small enough to fit in your pocket, but it's fun enough to keep you occupied for a good part of the day. I take the Game Boy and a handful of games anytime we go to my in-laws, but especially for their dreary daylong parties. The Game Boy even comes with headphones to further help you drown out the festivities. The main thing to remember, though, is to bring your battery charger with you. If you run out of juice, you might have to talk to someone, heaven forbid.

—K.O.
NEWTON FALLS, OHIO
YEARS WITH IN-LAWS: 6

GROUNDS FOR DIVORCE II

In 2005, a Romanian woman filed for divorce on the grounds that she could no longer tolerate having lunch with her mother-in-law every day.

IF YOUR MOTHER-IN-LAW IS A DRINKER, sit back and watch her drink all the Chardonnay she wants so she eventually passes out at 8 p.m. Politely set the table for dinner and do the dishes so it doesn't distract from her continuous boozing. For two hours, you will have to suffer while she says offensive things and talks inarticulately about politics and the war. She will complain about how much stress she has: She has to choose the perfect floors, paint, and hardware for her new condo. Pretend you are paying close attention by nodding your head and smiling, and silently pray that your partner never ends up like her. You will be pissed off, but remember, it is only temporary.

> —S.K.
> SAN DIEGO, CALIFORNIA

• • • • • • • •

IN MY WIFE'S FAMILY, get-togethers entail all the men hanging out in front of the television and all the women sitting around the dining-room table, gossiping. Call me crazy, but the gossip is more interesting than the football or basketball game the men are watching. Very few men know this, because they never give it a try. It's like watching a soap opera unfold right before your eyes. Next time you are in that situation, drag yourself away from the television, get some popcorn, and listen to the women talk about their friends.

> —FRED MATHEIS
> DEERFIELD, OHIO
> YEARS WITH IN-LAWS: 42

IT'S THOUGHTFUL TO BRING FLOWERS or wine for your in-laws when they invite you over for a nice dinner. I know it may not always be possible, but they'll notice such a nice gesture when you do.

—MICHAEL NOBLE
TORONTO, CANADA

• • • • • • • •

IF YOU'RE LUCKY, your wife's family will have a game room or something like that where you can hang out when you need to get away for a little while. When he still lived at home, my wife's brother turned his parents' basement into a nice little space for men only, with a bar, pool table, and television. I just head down there when I need to get away. If your in-laws don't have something like that, maybe you should start building one.

—MICHAEL GIULIANO
HUBBARD, OHIO
YEARS WITH IN-LAWS: 24

• • • • • • • •

WHEN VISITING YOUR IN-LAWS, be seen but not heard. They'll be happy that you showed up, and you can keep yourself out of hot water by keeping your mouth shut. My mother always said that's why God gave us one mouth and two ears.

—SUE LASKY
POLAND, OHIO
YEARS WITH IN-LAWS: 26

MY WIFE HAS THREE BROTHERS AND SISTERS, and they are all married. So whenever we all get together, the other three in-laws and I hang out together and commiserate about the wacky family we married into. We'll be talking on the porch, and one of our spouses will come out, and we'll say, "Sorry, you have to leave, this is an in-laws meeting." Misery loves company, so it's nice to suffer through those parties with others in the same situation.

I'll have Michael's brother-in-law prep me!

—ARCHIE WEIL
PRICETOWN, OHIO
YEARS WITH IN-LAWS: 1

• • • • • • • •

ENJOY FAMILY GET-TOGETHERS with your in-laws. My mother-in-law is 89 years old and lives five doors away from us. She's fun, she's sharp as a tack, and she's got a good sense of humor. She's there, and it's no problem, because she doesn't leave the house by herself. It's especially great for my husband, because he can stop by all the time. And if I see his car there, I'll stop and visit. Her sister lives in town, too, so sometimes we'll have "the girls" over. And when they get together, it's a riot.

—M. Z. THWAITE WEEKS
RIVERTON, NEW JERSEY
YEARS WITH IN-LAWS: 3

IT'S ALL ABOUT THE FOOD

THE WORST THING ABOUT GETTING together at my in-laws' house (and they were always inviting us over) was having dinner with them. My mother-in-law used awful recipes. She thought the recipes were very clever, and she would do things like boil a pork roast for an hour and a half while we were at church. Then she would slap it on a dish and pour a jar of barbecue sauce over it. It was terrible! I learned to try to arrange get-togethers at restaurants or to do noneating things like go to the movies together.

—S.B.
SOUTH BEND, INDIANA
YEARS WITH IN-LAWS: 5

• • • • • • • •

MY WIFE'S PARENTS ARE FANTASTIC COOKS. Her mom makes this flan that is famous even in Little Havana. Her father is also an amazing chef. So when they cooked, I would eat seconds and thirds of everything they served. They loved that a lot. That was absolutely the way to their heart, to enjoy their food and want more and more of it. Eat the food they give you. And then ask for seconds, and when they offer thirds, go for that as well.

—ANONYMOUS
ATLANTA, GEORGIA
YEARS WITH IN-LAWS: 16

MY MOTHER-IN-LAW THINKS she can cook. She made a dish with deer, and I swear the deer would've died when he saw how she prepared it—if he hadn't been dead already.

—SAVANNAH JORDAN
MONTAGUE, MICHIGAN
YEARS WITH IN-LAWS: 13

• • • • • • • •

WHEN YOUR MOTHER-IN-LAW comes to stay and suggests that she cook a pie, brats, homemade chicken soup, lasagna from scratch, and a handful of other dishes for her son, confidently and with purpose reply, "Oh yes, that sounds great!" It takes practice, but you'll get there.

—J.P.
SEATTLE, WASHINGTON
YEARS WITH IN-LAWS: 6

• • • • • • • •

MY MOTHER-IN-LAW DOESN'T USE seasoning in anything she cooks. Not ever! We live several hours apart, so we usually spend the weekend with them when we visit. My husband will make up some excuse for us to leave the house, to do an errand or to go for a ride somewhere, so we can get something to eat.

—ANONYMOUS
INDIANAPOLIS, INDIANA
YEARS WITH IN-LAWS: 10

BE OPEN TO THE WAY OTHER FAMILIES do things, even down to the type of milk they drink.

—B. J. KLINCK
PLYMOUTH, MINNESOTA
YEARS WITH IN-LAWS: 1

• • • • • • • •

I'M LUCKY TO HAVE FLEXIBLE IN-LAWS. When I was first getting to know them, my in-laws served bluefish for dinner, and they were so excited to have it. Unfortunately, I hate it. I pushed it around on the plate, until finally my mother-in-law noticed. She came over to me and said privately, "Would you like me to make you some chicken?" Whenever possible, be yourself; be honest.

—SUZY
WEST CALDWELL, NEW JERSEY
YEARS WITH IN-LAWS: 10

• • • • • • • •

IF YOUR MOTHER-IN-LAW THINKS she is a good cook, always appreciate it, no matter what you really think. Nothing can sting your husband quite like insulting his mother's cooking.

—RUTH
BURLINGAME, CALIFORNIA
YEARS WITH IN-LAWS: 25

I PRAISE MY MOTHER-IN-LAW'S COOKING all the time. Secretly, I don't think she's such a great cook. But she tries, and she thinks of herself as a real gourmet, so what's the harm in making her feel appreciated?

—C.S.
SAN FRANCISCO, CALIFORNIA
YEARS WITH IN-LAWS: 3

• • • • • • • •

MY MOTHER-IN-LAW is a fantastic cook; she studied in France! But all her best dishes are loaded with cream and butter, and really bad for me. Hmmm . . . I wonder if . . .

—N.K.
NEW YORK, NEW YORK
YEARS WITH IN-LAWS: 22

> *I feel like we're all mixed nuts.*

WHEN MY HUSBAND'S FAMILY DESCENDS, they have that family thing going, and I'm not part of it. I always feel like an apple in a room full of oranges. I've given up on trying to change that, and instead I just focus on getting through it. It also helps to remind myself that when my family visits, the shoe's going to be on the other foot.

—ANONYMOUS
BOULDER, COLORADO
YEARS WITH IN-LAWS: 4

. . . .

IT REALLY HELPS IF YOU CAN CONNECT with another "out-law." I remember, for example, the first time I attended a big family dinner with my future in-laws. I was sitting next to another girlfriend, who has since become my sister-in-law, and we were having a great time talking until my now-husband said, kind of sternly, "Mary, my dad is talking." We were really surprised, and then I realized that at his family's dinner table, his dad really held court, and everyone else would just listen and not talk. And we hadn't realized that, because in our own families, everybody talked around the dinner table at the same time. Since then, my sister-in-law and I have gotten through a lot of family events and outings by being able to connect with each other and process the weird family dynamics together.

—MARY
ST. PAUL, MINNESOTA
YEARS WITH IN-LAWS: 15

MY MOTHER-IN-LAW IS A CONTROL FREAK. Over the years, I have been the one to voice my opinion when she's being unreasonable, and my husband has just stood by. I've told my husband, though, that it would be more effective if he, as the family member, would speak up. I believed that his mother would hear things, especially critical things, better from him. My husband has started to do this, and it has helped a lot.

> *Always better to speak to your own parent.*

> —ANONYMOUS
> EASTON, PENNSYLVANIA
> YEARS WITH IN-LAWS: 13

• • • • • • • •

I WAS INITIALLY SHY AT FAMILY get-togethers. My husband's family is much louder and more vocal than mine; I found that overwhelming. At some point, it occurred to me that I was feeling left out because I was keeping myself on the sidelines. It was my attitude, not their treatment of me. The easiest way for me to get comfortable is to do something: clear the table, talk to the kids, take pictures. Also, this is a family that loves to laugh, and once we're laughing, we've definitely bonded.

Consider

> —ANDREA
> PHILADELPHIA, PENNSYLVANIA
> YEARS WITH IN-LAWS: 15

OUR WHOLE FAMILY WENT OUT to eat at Bob's Big Boy, and my father-in-law ate so much that he unbuckled his pants at the table and started burping and farting and saying, "Better out than in! Better out than in!" My kids, who were teenagers at the time, were mortified, but the more they asked him to stop, the more he did it. He had done this before around the dinner table, but never in a restaurant. I'd known since I met him that he was a pig, and I worried that my husband would have similar behavior. I was always on the lookout. The best thing to do in a situation like this is to get up, walk away, and not feed into it. Talking to the person might be an option, but with my father-in-law, anything we said fell on deaf ears.

—LINDA
PORT JEFFERSON, NEW YORK
YEARS WITH IN-LAWS: 30

• • • • • • • •

I guess I shouldn't worry too much about coffee.

MY HUSBAND'S FAMILY ARE REALLY heavy drinkers, to the point where they will get drunk and not remember what happened. My family, on the other hand, will only have the occasional beer. One night, we all went out to an Indian restaurant. My in-laws kept refilling my mom's wineglass, she got drunk, and they were making fun of her. Sometimes I don't think it's good to get the in-laws together.

—ANGELA
WAKE FOREST, NORTH CAROLINA
YEARS WITH IN-LAWS: 8

SEX AT YOUR IN-LAWS'?

HAVING SEX IN YOUR IN-LAWS' HOUSE is a huge taboo—the first time you visit, and every time thereafter. My wife had a strict Catholic upbringing; her mother goes to mass every day and helps count the money afterward. We definitely can't do it in the room she grew up in. There's just something about the thin, squeaky beds and the fear of getting caught. However, if her parents leave for church, and we don't go, there's a one-hour window of opportunity.

—DOUG BRIMMER
COLORADO SPRINGS, COLORADO
YEARS WITH IN-LAWS: 13

• • • • • • • •

WHEN WE STAYED WITH MY WIFE'S FATHER before we were married, I would have to sleep on the couch. I think it was hard for him to have us sleep in the same room, even after we were married. I think it's just too weird for a daughter to have sex knowing that her dad's thinking, "I hope my daughter isn't in there screwing." And the daughter's thinking, "That's what my dad is thinking, and here I am screwing. I'm letting him down! I'm no longer Daddy's little girl!" It was frustrating; you go on vacation with the in-laws and you have less sex, and vacation is when you're supposed to be having more sex.

—S.H.
ATLANTA, GEORGIA
YEARS WITH IN-LAWS: 10

WE ALWAYS GO TO VISIT MY IN-LAWS. That way, we maintain the control over when we arrive and when we leave. And instead of staying at their home, we get a hotel room. That way, we have a place to escape to!

—ANONYMOUS
ALLENTOWN, PENNSYLVANIA
YEARS WITH IN-LAWS: 17

. . . .

> There's a lot to be said for keeping cool under pressure.

GET-TOGETHERS WITH MY FATHER-IN-LAW were very tense. He was so controlling and domineering. I kept my cool and waited until my wife and I got in the car and drove away before getting it all out. If you know you are in it for the long run, you have to make every effort to accept everything about your partner, even her parents. If you have problems with your in-laws, do everything you can to work them out.

—BARRY GREENE
LOS ANGELES, CALIFORNIA
YEARS WITH IN-LAWS: 10

. . . .

I HAVE HAD TO LAY DOWN THE LAW when it came to my mother-in-law visiting—two days, max. More than that, and I start to go crazy. I can deal with her for a couple of days, and we get along fine. But after that, the ice starts getting pretty thin. It's best for all involved to keep visits short and sweet.

—ANONYMOUS
ATLANTA, GEORGIA

TRY TO INCORPORATE NEW IN-LAWS into some of your own family traditions, especially those that you think are fun. For example, in my husband's family, there is a tradition that each time red wine is spilt at the dinner table, everyone needs to get some of the wine rubbed on their forehead and say the word *alegria*, which means "happiness" in Spanish. Although this is a little weird for newcomers, they instantly feel like they are part of something special.

—RUTH
BURLINGAME, CALIFORNIA
YEARS WITH IN-LAWS: 25

• • • • • • • •

MY WIFE'S DAD JUST MOVED to the Philippines four months ago, but he was living with us the whole year before that. He'd call my wife every afternoon and say, "What's for dinner?" My wife was stressing. She felt like she was cooking for two husbands. And he'd just sit and watch TV, turning it up as loud as he needed, no matter what was going on around him. I learned to stay out of the way and let my wife work it out. I like it better when my mother-in-law visits. She cleans out the fridge and does all the laundry. We encourage it.

—ANONYMOUS
BURLINGTON, NORTH CAROLINA
YEARS WITH IN-LAWS: 13

THE NICEST THING MY IN-LAWS DID FOR ME

THEY HELP US WHEN WE MOVE. They've helped us pack and then organize our new homes, even when we moved to Europe. And they never tell me how our home should be organized; my best friends don't even do that!

—LORRAINE BRANCATTO BOERSMA
TOLEDO, OHIO
YEARS WITH IN-LAWS: 8

• • • • • • • •

THEY MOVED FROM VIRGINIA (where we lived) to Florida. We rarely had to see them. They were nice, but we needed the space to grow up on our own. And they also sold their house to us for a good price.

—ANONYMOUS
WILLIAMSBURG, VIRGINIA
YEARS WITH IN-LAWS: 34

• • • • • • • •

THE BEST THING MY MOTHER-IN-LAW ever did for me was to take my side. Always. I always felt that there was someone in my corner. She's 86 years old and still asks me if her son is treating me right.

—PAGET PERRAULT
MELBOURNE, AUSTRALIA
YEARS WITH IN-LAWS: 36

THEY GAVE US THE DOWN PAYMENT on a house. This was difficult for them because they knew we were looking at a home that was far away from them. But they accepted our decision and helped us begin our life together in a beautiful home. We make sure to invite them to our home often.

—L.C.
PITTSBURGH, PENNSYLVANIA
YEARS WITH IN-LAWS: 12

• • • • • • • • •

WE BOUGHT A HOUSE way out of town. Almost immediately after the closing we realized we had to stay in the city. Then housing prices plummeted. We rented it to students, who trashed the place and dealt drugs. My father-in-law stepped in and managed the property for us until we could sell it, about eight years later. He said, "I'm going to make lemonade out of this!" He did.

—C.F.
BROOKLYN, NEW YORK
YEARS WITH IN-LAWS: 25

I GET ALONG PRETTY WELL with my in-laws, but it doesn't hurt that they live six hours away and we only see them once a year.

—ANONYMOUS
ALLENTOWN, PENNSYLVANIA
YEARS WITH IN-LAWS: 17

• • • • • • • •

WHEN MY HUSBAND AND I were first married, it would really bug me when his family would impose upon us. It caused quite a lot of arguments. Then I realized that if my husband had asked, it wouldn't have upset me a bit, because I was doing it for him instead of for them. Now, when my husband's family asks me for something, I respond as if my husband is doing the asking. That way I feel that I am doing something nice for *him*, which is always a pleasure.

> *I like this woman's thinking.*

—KRISTEN
BETHLEHEM, PENNSYLVANIA
YEARS WITH IN-LAWS: 9

• • • • • • • •

AVOID THEIR HOT-BUTTON ISSUES: Early on I learned that there are some things that set off my mother-in-law. If she isn't served first at a party, for instance, or on just the right plate, she feels slighted and gets upset. Over the years, as I've realized what types of things upset her, I've been careful to avoid doing them.

—ANONYMOUS
DUBOIS, PENNSYLVANIA
YEARS WITH IN-LAWS: 22

WE VISIT MY MOTHER-IN-LAW and her husband in California every other year or so. But that can be tricky because it's also our family vacation, and I don't want to spend all our time with his folks. One time, we spent a couple of days with them and then drove up the coast to stay at a really nice resort. When we got there, there was a note from them at the front desk: They had decided to come to the resort, too, and had checked into the room right next to us!

—MARY
ST. PAUL, MINNESOTA

• • • • • • • • •

MY FATHER-IN-LAW IS QUITE a difficult man. When he came to visit us last year, he gave us one day's notice, but we quickly made adjustments. From the moment that he walked in the door, he complained about the weather, the house, our son—whatever he could think of. He was supposed to stay for three weeks, but he kept saying that he was too busy to visit us anyway, so he would probably leave sooner than expected. He actually did leave four days later, so quickly that he still had clothes in the dryer when his cab came to take him to the airport. I wasn't sad to see him go. But I was sad for my wife because she had tried so hard to make the last-minute trip so nice for him. He still talks about coming back to visit us, but he'll have to ask me first!

Good rule: Give notice before a visit.

—J.K.
SWEDEN
YEARS WITH IN-LAWS: 7

WHEN IN HARARE . . .

Everyone has something interesting to say about in-laws, it seems. Recently, while I was having a pedicure, I heard a story from Grace, the esthetician. Grace, who is from Zimbabwe, told me that in her culture, a woman is expected to stay with her in-laws when she travels home. I didn't really understand her: "So, you visit your in-laws when you go home to Africa?" I said.

"No", Grace responded, "I visit *my* family from my in-laws' house when I travel back to Africa. And my father and siblings live in a different town, so I don't get to spend too much time with them. But in our society it would be considered rude and inappropriate to stay with my side." Grace has avoided traveling back home because it's too stressful to try to squeeze her family into the plans. I couldn't believe it: I imagined how different our relationship to our in-laws would be if we adopted this tradition. In a difficult situation, but one where there's little choice in the matter, would we simply do our best to have a solid and respectable relationship with our in-laws?

Grace also told me that there's a wedding tradition in which the bride travels from town to town to meet all of her new in-laws. She is seated in the center of the room while her new family dances around her and gives her gifts, treats, and money. Now, that sounds more like it!

EVEN IF MONEY IS TIGHT, always offer to put your mother-in-law up in a hotel near your home. Avoid having her stay with you; no good can come from that!

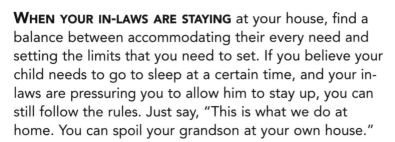

> —ANONYMOUS
> NEW YORK, NEW YORK

• • • • • • • •

WHEN YOUR IN-LAWS ARE STAYING at your house, find a balance between accommodating their every need and setting the limits that you need to set. If you believe your child needs to go to sleep at a certain time, and your in-laws are pressuring you to allow him to stay up, you can still follow the rules. Just say, "This is what we do at home. You can spoil your grandson at your own house."

> —RUTH
> BURLINGAME, CALIFORNIA
> YEARS WITH IN-LAWS: 25

• • • • • • • •

MY MOTHER-IN-LAW IS THE KIND of person who comes to dinner and takes over your kitchen. After years of frustration and arguments, I finally hit upon a solution: Before she arrives, I come up with a list of tasks that I feel comfortable delegating to her. For example, I might ask her to cut up the vegetables and set the table. This makes my mother-in-law feel useful, and it keeps her busy and out of my hair.

What's the problem with that?

> —ANONYMOUS
> EASTON, PENNSYLVANIA
> YEARS WITH IN-LAWS: 13

MY IN-LAWS USED TO COME over every Sunday, and I'd cook for them and serve them. Since I didn't have a good relationship with them, I started to get annoyed with this routine. One Sunday I told my husband to tell his parents that we couldn't get together. My mother-in-law's reply was, "It's OK—we won't stay long." So I left the house. I went about my day, since I felt they imposed themselves on me and didn't listen to me. This made them upset, but I had to do this.

—DEE DEE MELMET
SONOMA, CALIFORNIA
YEARS WITH IN-LAWS: 10

• • • • • • • • •

Help with laundry and cooking will never offend me.

MY HUSBAND'S MOTHER LOVES to do the cooking, cleaning, and laundry at our house. When we were first married, I wouldn't let her help, because I didn't want her to think that I was incapable or lazy. But she became very unhappy, was moody, and didn't say a word to anyone. My mom told me to give her a load of laundry and tell her to cook something. She is not the kind of woman who sits and socializes with company; she would rather work. This is what I did, and it made a world of difference. She was fun, she told stories, and she was laughing and happy once I gave her lots of tasks.

—PATTY LAMBROPOULOS
LAKE FOREST, ILLINOIS

MY IN-LAWS JUST CAME TO STAY with us for six weeks. They're from Australia, so they think as long as they've traveled so far, they may as well stay a while. After a long history of trouble, dating back to when they tried to prevent our marriage, I decided to look at them as if meeting them for the first time. Without the baggage of the past, their annoying traits and interfering ways were much easier to cope with. When the situation had the potential to become really bad, I chose to ignore and divert, much like I do with my toddler!

—MICHELLE LAPAGLIA
LOS ANGELES, CALIFORNIA

• • • • • • • •

IN-LAWS SHOULD NEVER DROP in unexpectedly. One of my coworkers had a lot of burglaries in his neighborhood. One night, he was sitting at home drinking a beer when his father-in-law walked in unexpectedly. The guy was so startled, he threw the loaded beer can at his father-in-law, who, needless to say, wasn't happy about that. But honestly, what did the guy expect? His son-in-law assumed he was a burglar!

Yes! Tell your in-laws that unexpected visits are dangerous.

—JOE HOLLIMAN
CENTENNIAL, COLORADO
YEARS WITH IN-LAWS: 33

MY IN-LAWS LIVED WITH US for three months while they looked for a house in our area. Because of the tension in the house, I found myself clamming up and keeping to myself when I got home from work. My solution, and I admit it wasn't the best one, was to drink a Manhattan every night. That allowed me to open up and be social and survive the three long months.

—BARBARA LAVALETTE
RALEIGH, NORTH CAROLINA
YEARS WITH IN-LAWS: 4

• • • • • • • •

I HAVE A BROTHER-IN-LAW WHO is 6 feet 4 inches tall and weighs 250 pounds. When he comes over, he eats like a cow, shoveling food in with his hands. When he sits down, he just falls into his seat. On a number of occasions, he has broken our furniture. One night, after a hearty meal, he fell onto our couch and broke the leg. His reaction was just "Oops." He came over again when we were having a barbecue, sat at the picnic table, and broke the supporting beam. Our solution is to have plastic furniture so that if it breaks when he sits on it, it's no big deal. We all sit on dining-room furniture, and he's on plastic.

—ANONYMOUS
PISCATAWAY, NEW JERSEY
YEARS WITH IN-LAWS: 19

FRANCIS THE TALKING PARROT-IN-LAW

It's a bird ... it's a gun ... it's my ex-boyfriend's parents' house! Visiting my prospective in-laws was a warning from the future. I remember that his father picked us up from the airport and said, "Here they are—in from California, where they live with the fruits and the nuts!" He thought we were crazy for liking the West Coast and teased me for my liberal politics. I felt itchy. Aren't you supposed to avoid topics like politics and religion with people you hardly know? He showed me his collection of guns. I felt itchy again.

Now I know what that itchy feeling was really about. It's a common psychosomatic reaction to in-laws, one that's been confirmed by medical research. Rashes, migraine headaches, the flu ... had I known then about "in-law syndrome," I would have taken the next flight back to California.

These people were very kind, and as sweet as the pie his mom made, but I had a hard time relating. They lived with a parrot, who barked at the dog all day and answered the phone (to himself) when it rang, in a perfect imitation of my boyfriend's mother. She'd pick up the phone and the parrot would echo, "Hello. Well, hi there!" To me, the parrot offered a satirical comment on the whole family, waking us every morning, and screaming for half the day. I got the message.

THE FIRST TIME MY HUSBAND and I spent the night at his parents' house, two of his siblings and their spouses were also visiting. Because there weren't enough bedrooms to accommodate all the married couples, my mother-in-law had the girls sleep in one room, and the boys in another. My husband ended up snoring so badly that his brother-in-law got up and went to sleep in the laundry room; we couldn't find him in the morning! Get a hotel room, because that's the only way you'll have privacy. I used to think the idea of not staying with family was appalling, but it's the only way you'll be able to do what you like. Besides, you can visit every single day if you want.

> *Isn't that why they invented hotels?*

—CHERI HURD
LITTLETON, COLORADO
YEARS WITH IN-LAWS: 32

. . . .

IF YOU'RE GOING TO SPEND a weekend at your parents' or in-laws' house, make sure you and your spouse have alone time. It's easy to get swallowed up in the family dynamic, so schedule afternoon walks in the woods or something like that to regain yourselves. When we're at my folks' place, my husband and I walk to my elementary school and shoot hoops.

—ANONYMOUS
ST. LOUIS, MISSOURI
YEARS WITH IN-LAWS: 1

DON'T BE CORNERED ALONE, especially near photo albums! I once got caught hearing hours of stories from my mother-in-law about how bad and disrespectful my husband was. How should one respond? Agree with her? Laugh? I decided to take the safe route and politely nod.

—LISA DOUGLASS
SAN FRANCISCO, CALIFORNIA
YEARS WITH IN-LAWS: 1

· · · · · · · ·

MY FIRST HUSBAND'S FATHER was a pathologist; he conducted autopsies. He and his wife were big drinkers. One day, we went to their place for an outdoor party. They were using an autopsy table as their bar. I was mortified. The table tilted a little, so if any booze was spilled, it ran down the table into a bucket.

Whoa!

—ANONYMOUS
INDIANAPOLIS, INDIANA
YEARS WITH IN-LAWS: 10

· · · · · · · · ·

MY WIFE'S MOM VISITS for two weeks at a time. I've started taking the lead to do something fun with her so I don't always feel like she's invading my turf. We'll go to a museum in town that features a painter she likes. That way, I have something to be excited about instead of feeling sorry for myself that she's here again for two weeks.

—TOM FISHBURNE
MINNEAPOLIS, MINNESOTA
YEARS WITH IN-LAWS: 5

MY HUSBAND'S BROTHER, mom, and dad came to visit; they were all staying at our house. One night, all five of us were cooking supper. His brother got the placemats out and set four places at the table. They all sat down and started to serve the food, and I just kind of stood there—there was no place for me to sit. That was the last time they stayed here.

—JENNIFER
LAS VEGAS, NEVADA
YEARS WITH IN-LAWS: 20

Happy, Merry, and Thankful: Surviving the Holidays

Whenever I spend a holiday with my in-laws, I add to my store of culinary knowledge in one particular category—I am introduced to a food I don't recognize, stuffed. Artichokes, grape leaves, zucchini—you name it, my mother-in-law stuffs it.

My own mother is a fantastic cook and I have never asked her to share a recipe: this is a clue to my level of interest in cooking. But I see that bonding over food may be a good way to connect with my future mother-in-law. I have a strong sense that there will be stuffing in my future, since that is what my soon-to-be-husband expects to

*see on his holiday dinner table. I could tell him to "stuff
it," but I figure I should roll up my sleeves, ask my mother-
in-law to share her talent, and learn the art of stuffing.
Who knows? Besides bringing a little bit of their house
into ours, I may find a new food to stuff. Grape, peapod,
pomegranate, anyone?*

*Many people we interviewed for this book felt that it
was important to establish their own family traditions.
Some choose to reserve a day during the holidays for
their nuclear family to establish new rituals and find time
to connect among themselves.*

*Whatever you do, try to find a balance between your
in-laws' holiday rituals—no matter how strange they may
be—and the way you would ideally do it. This way, you
will not feel that you have given up the whole holiday
participating in activities that have little or no meaning
for you.*

MY EX-MOTHER-IN-LAW WOULD BUY Christmas gifts for my husband, our daughter, and me all year long. She always showed them to us, talked about how she got them on sale, and then piled them in plain sight in their extra bedroom. At Christmas, she wrapped them, as if they'd be a surprise. I didn't know what to do, so I just went along with it, or said things like, "Well, I finally get to use this. Thank you, Shirley." Her husband would always say, "Oh, she's crazy. You don't have to pretend like you don't know what it is." It was really, really awkward.

—S.B.
SOUTH BEND, INDIANA
YEARS WITH IN-LAWS: 5

• • • • • • • •

MY FAMILY AND MY IN-LAWS never got along. It made holidays really stressful. I always loved Christmas until I got married, and when we had kids I had to figure out a way to take the holiday back so I didn't become one of those parents who are always grumpy and mean at Christmas. I had to give up being with my family every second year, which was sad for me. But it was better than the extreme discomfort of having our parents in the same room.

—PETER STEUR
BRISBANE, AUSTRALIA
YEARS WITH IN-LAWS: 6

> When all else fails, compromise.

COOKING FOR THE JEWISH HOLIDAYS is great fun. Usually, my husband never cooks with me, but massive amounts of chicken seem to be required for these meals. He takes over all the chicken recipes. I also know that the people in his family are notoriously bad cooks, so I don't feel pressured. His relatives are always appreciative; in fact, they're blown away.

> —M.M.
> PHILADELPHIA, PENNSYLVANIA

MY IN-LAWS EAT PICKLED ham at Christmas, and the whole family loves pickled ham. I think it's disgusting. The first holiday, my husband didn't tell me about this custom, so I tried it and smiled and knew I wouldn't eat any more. That was the last time I ate it, and that was nine or ten years ago.

> —ANONYMOUS
> DES MOINES, IOWA
> YEARS WITH IN-LAWS: 11

DARK AND CREEPY

Mother-in-Law Day is always celebrated on the fourth Sunday in October, along with the end of Daylight Saving Time and the approach of Halloween.

FOOD FOR THE FOODIES

MY MOTHER-IN-LAW'S FAILURES in the kitchen were legendary. We once stopped by for a Wednesday-night Thanksgiving meal on our way to my own parents' house, but my husband insisted that we treat her to a nice dinner out—at the Olive Garden. This, I was quick to learn, was the only way to escape the unknown dangers lurking in her kitchen.

After so many years, however, our reluctance to eat in had become not only suspicious, but borderline rude. One Christmas we decided that our treat for her would be to cook an extravagant meal straight from the pages of *Gourmet*. We carted half our kitchen plus every single ingredient in the trunk of our car and cooked for an entire day. The meal was spectacular. We were exhausted by the end of it. My mother-in-law was left with so much food she probably had to throw most of it away. Since then, I've set aside my food snobbery when we visit. As my husband said of his years in her home, "I didn't die, you know."

—JENNIFER
SHEBOYGAN, WISCONSIN
YEARS WITH IN-LAWS: 1

IN-LAW FOLLIES #4

IT WAS CHRISTMAS EVE. The in-laws were visiting our house. We also had another visitor: a mouse that had been ransacking our pantry but slipping through my system of mousetraps. I had been using no-kill traps, the kind where the mouse gets inside and can't get back out until you release him outside, far away. Well, after dinner and the gift opening, everyone was settling in, I decided to check the trap in the pantry. The peanut butter was gone, but the trap seemed empty. I brought the trap out to the living room, where everyone was gathered. "Look," I said. "It seems like a mouse was in here, but now he's gone." At this point, the mouse, somehow hiding out of sight, leapt from the trap into the middle of the party, scampering for his life. If done on purpose, it would have made a great practical joke; everyone freaked out. The mouse ran for a corner and disappeared into a cabinet and the wall. Then, everyone started laughing at me. Later, when we read "The Night Before Christmas" to the kids, the line "no creature was stirring, not even a mouse," elicited laughs. When something like this happens, you just have to accept the fact that you have entered the book of family lore, and your story will be retold for generations.

—J.W.A.
ATLANTA, GEORGIA
YEARS WITH IN-LAWS: 10

IF YOU LIVE FAR AWAY FROM YOUR IN-LAWS, and the holidays are about the only time you see them, the experience will be much better if you keep in close touch with them during the year.

—BECKY LAKE
BADEN, PENNSYLVANIA
YEARS WITH IN-LAWS: 22

IN-LAWS ON THE SMALL SCREEN

Who shot J.R.? His sister-in-law, of course. The famous television whodunit is but one instance in which in-laws have clashed on the small screen. While you're considering your relationship with your sister-in-law (and whether or not she owns a gun), here are a few favorite TV shows that exploited the challenging in-law dynamic as a setup for plotlines and punch lines.

The Addams Family
   (1964-1966)

All in the Family
   (1971-1979)

The Beverly Hillbillies
   (1962-1971)

Bewitched
   (1964-1972)

Dallas
   (1978-1991)

Everybody Loves Raymond
   (1996-2005)

The Flintstones
   (1960-1966)

The Munsters
   (1964-1966)

Roseanne
   (1988-1997)

Soap
   (1977-1981)

IT'S THE THOUGHT THAT COUNTS, RIGHT?

A 24-INCH-HIGH GREEN BAY PACKERS light-up fleece-covered snowman that waves his hand. Enough said!

—J.P.
SEATTLE, WASHINGTON
YEARS WITH IN-LAWS: 6

• • • • • • • • •

I HAD A PAIR OF COW-SHAPED salt shakers in my kitchen that prompted my husband's family to assume that I loved cows. Over that next year, for Christmas, my birthday, and my college graduation, every gift that I received had a cow theme. Cow dish towels, a cow oven mitt, cow kitchen mats, cow T-shirts, cow barrettes, a cow soap dish, a cow lotion dispenser, a cow cookie jar, cow plates, cow cups, and a teakettle shaped like a cow. I didn't have the heart to tell them that my favorite animal was actually the pig.

—CECELIA REEVES
CHICO, CALIFORNIA
YEARS WITH IN-LAWS: 11

• • • • • • • • •

MY MOTHER-IN-LAW GAVE me all of her old underwear.

—M. D. E.
COLUMBIA, MISSOURI
YEARS WITH IN-LAWS: 30

MY MOTHER-IN-LAW HAS A KNACK for giving bizarre, crappy gifts. For my son's birthday, she gave him an oar—a single oar! He doesn't even have a boat! She gave me a toilet-paper cover with a roll of toilet paper inside. It was this pink, tan, and black cow with a huge stuffed head, these fat outstretched arms, and a giant billowy skirt that hid the roll. I mean, c'mon! This was a Christmas gift. My sister-in-law was watching me unwrap it, and she was giving me this look, like, "It's OK. It's all right. Take it steady. Keep it low." I didn't know at the time that she had gotten the same thing. I snuck the cow cover into my daughter's luggage when she packed for college. At least I was keeping it in the family.

—BONNIE
FLORAL PARK, NEW YORK
YEARS WITH IN-LAWS: 36

• • • • • • • •

MY IN-LAWS ONCE GAVE US matching Western-style plaid shirts with snaps. Another time, my mother-in-law bought us, without asking first, a used china hutch *and* the china that went with it. I didn't want to hurt her feelings. At first I put china in it; then after I while I put books on it. I would never say, "No, we don't want it."

—ANONYMOUS
SEATTLE, WASHINGTON
YEARS WITH IN-LAWS: 28

LIVE WITH A GIFT YOU DON'T LOVE for at least a year to make the giver happy. After that, have a story ready for the disappearance of the object. My mother-in-law gave us a ceramic statue of a disheveled man holding a liquor bottle, coming through a door to a woman holding a rolling pin up in the air. When she gave it to us, she said to my husband, "Don't ever do this to your wife or you'll get bopped on the head with a rolling pin." We initially thought the statue was funny, but we also took it seriously because it was close to home: It was her way of reminding her son not to drink and cheat on me, which was what her husband did to her. We got tired of the statue pretty quickly and kept moving it from room to room because we couldn't find the right place for it. Eventually we stored it in the basement, and when she came to visit, I'd have to dig it out.

—ANONYMOUS
EASTON, PENNSYLVANIA
YEARS WITH IN-LAWS: 20

• • • • • • • •

MY IN-LAWS BOUGHT THIS HIDEOUS throw rug for my dining room that I keep in the basement. I only bring it out when I know they're coming over. That way everybody is happy, and I can keep the peace.

—ANONYMOUS
STRONGSVILLE, OHIO

THE NICEST THING THAT MY IN-LAWS ever did was to make a surprise visit during the Christmas holidays. They showed up one evening with food, cookies, eggnog, and presents. My wife and I, my sister and her husband, and my in-laws spent a wonderful evening listening to music, eating, and opening presents. Everyone had a great time. Sometimes, surprise visits can be the most fun and memorable!

Sweet!

—ANONYMOUS
WAIKOLOA, HAWAII
YEARS WITH IN-LAWS: 5

• • • • • • • •

BEFORE OUR FIRST THANKSGIVING together, I was unaware of the traditions in my husband's family. For instance, the women served the men and waited to eat until after the men were done. I just grabbed a plate and plopped down in an empty seat at the heavily laden table. As I started to sip the super-sweet iced tea, I noticed that the table had fallen silent, and all eyes were on me. I then noticed that I was not only the only woman at the table, but the only woman in the room! My husband took me aside and explained the old-fashioned traditions of his southern family. I thought it was ridiculous and silly, and I told him so. I was forgiven. However, I don't recall another segregated Thanksgiving.

—SHELLEY
TAMPA, FLORIDA
YEARS WITH IN-LAWS: 22

MATTERS OF TASTE

There are two kinds of gifts that in-laws bestow on their children: Family heirlooms and new (or re-gifted) items. An item that has been passed down in the family may be ugly or random, but it has emotional significance for your in-laws, and may be important to your spouse, or your children, in the future. It is a good idea to accept it with grace and appreciation. The other kind of gift—new stuff—reflects the giver's taste and is a little trickier to deal with.

My friend Jessica has asked her in-laws to call before stopping by. This is so she can bedeck her home with gifts given to her by her in-laws. She moves the "Beauty is in the Eye of the Beer Holder" mugs from her storage closet to the kitchen so she can serve her father-in-law a Bud in this classic vessel. Some would say she is perpetuating a bad gift-giving cycle, but I understand her conflict, as well as her solution.

I have never received a crocheted tea cozy, a hideous wall hanging, or any other random goody from the dollar store. My mother-in-law only buys thoughtful, lovely, and appropriate gifts. Many people I interviewed expressed horror at receiving in-law gifts that weren't to their taste. Some actually gave the item back, feeling that they are being direct and honest that way. Should it ever happen to me, I'll take Jessica's compromise—as long as I've got a large storage closet.

EACH YEAR MY FATHER-IN-LAW hosts a big family Christmas celebration. We've never gone, and we never will. Instead, my husband and I plan another day to spend with my father-in-law around the holidays. It's important to do what you want for yourself and for your spouse. If you go through life thinking, "I have to do this for my in-laws," or "My in-laws have to come over for this holiday," you will be miserable. Instead, seek out compromises. If you hate having your in-laws at your home, go to them or meet someplace.

—PAULA
WESTPORT, CONNECTICUT
YEARS WITH IN-LAWS: 5

• • • • • • • • •

FOR THE SAKE OF YOUR MARRIAGE and your family, it's important to create your own traditions. When we got married, both of our parents lived in town, and if we didn't immediately claim one holiday for ourselves, we might never be able to. We decided Thanksgiving would  be ours. We left town to prove how serious we were about being alone together, and it quickly became a tradition for the two of us to go away on Thanksgiving. When we had children, we started staying home on Thanksgiving and doing things together as a family, like playing board games, watching football, and having a fondue dinner. It's a special time for us.

—P.O.
NEW BRUNSWICK, NEW JERSEY
YEARS WITH IN-LAWS: 22

MY WIFE HAS A BIG FAMILY, and they make a big deal out of every birthday. Many of the birthdays fall between Thanksgiving and Christmas; there seems to be a party every other night. I decided one year that it would have to be OK if I didn't attend every single one. It was just too overwhelming. It's important to build our own traditions as a little family in addition to the bigger bashes.

—DAVID TRENT
WOODWORTH, OHIO
YEARS WITH IN-LAWS: 15

• • • • • • • •

MY WIFE HAD TWO SETS OF PARENTS, and they lived 100 miles apart from each other. However, when the holidays rolled around, we were expected to celebrate with both sets. It's a good thing I didn't have any contact with my parents, otherwise I don't know how we could have done it. For example, we had Christmas breakfast with one parent in Sherman Oaks, then drove 100 miles to Santa Barbara for Christmas Day, then back to Sherman Oaks for Christmas night. It was a drag, but I did it because I loved my wife.

Two sets of in-laws? Double the fun!

—BARRY GREENE
LOS ANGELES, CALIFORNIA
YEARS WITH IN-LAWS: 10

Mine! Your Kids, Their Grandkids

When I'm with my in-laws and their other grandchild I feel pressured. I want to look like the perfect prospective parent for my in-laws' future grandchildren, but I freeze when I am around my sister-in-law's baby. Oh, I can coo and talk baby talk, because I honestly think my sister-in-law's baby is adorable; but I do not know how to calm him or make him giggle when he's crying. How can I succeed as a mother if I am failing my duty as his aunt?

Even though I am not a baby person (I am always scared I'll drop the little bundle), I do want to have children; just not right away. I know that the moment I kick off my wedding shoes, my family-in-law will start talking about babies.

I have already seen that inquiring look, the one that says, "You and Michael will make beautiful children together. So, when?!"

Many respondents resent what they see as their in-laws' interference with the kids. But it's hard for me not to view the alternative—no family involvement; having to go it all alone—as perhaps a lonely one. I'm sure it can be difficult, but worthwhile, to find that middle ground.

Michael's family is good at making babies—I just hope they will be fine if Michael and I wait a few years before we add to their already massive family tree. Not only do I need plenty of time to get used to the idea of parenting, I'll need to prepare for countless aunts, uncles, and cousins telling me how best to do the job. Give me strength!

I THINK IT'S GOOD TO ESTABLISH some ground rules right at the start when your in-laws are taking care of your children. You can bet those rules are going to get bent by Grandma, but at least it's worth trying.

—ERICA GRAHAM
ACCIDENT, MARYLAND
YEARS WITH IN-LAWS: 3

• • • • • • • •

OUR SON STAYED OVERNIGHT with my in-laws, and when he came back, he was constantly talking about Jesus. He said Grandma had said that Jesus would be sitting over his bed every night when he slept. I thought that was kind of a creepy thought. But rather than getting all bothered about it, I decided I would say, "Well, this is what Grandma thinks, and that's OK, but I think about things this other way," and so forth.

—E.H.
MINNEAPOLIS, MINNESOTA
YEARS WITH IN-LAWS: 11

• • • • • • • •

THIS IS A GOOD EXAMPLE of Murphy's Law: When your in-laws babysit for your kids, and you are about three days from your next paycheck, it is inevitable that this is the day you will run out of milk, juice, snack foods, wipes, and diapers, all at once. It never fails. And you *will* hear about it.

—CECELIA REEVES
CHICO, CALIFORNIA
YEARS WITH IN-LAWS: 11

MY MOTHER-IN-LAW AND SISTER-IN-LAW once witnessed my four-year-old daughter break down in a nasty temper tantrum. About a week later, each called my husband to say that our daughter needed psychological help. I knew that all my daughter needed was love and understanding. I got very angry and resentful toward my husband. In retrospect, I should have called my in-laws to explain the situation. There is no need to drive a wedge between you and your spouse just because you resent what his family says. Communicating directly with your in-laws about issues can actually improve your relationship with them.

—GRACIELA SHOLANDER
FORT COLLINS, COLORADO

LETHAL IMPLICATIONS

In a study of German church records of the 18th century, evidence suggests that a mother-in-law may have had a fatal effect on her daughter-in-law's children: The chance of a child dying within a month of birth doubled if the child's paternal grandmother was alive. In contrast, maternal grandmothers greatly improved a child's prospects for survival in the first year. Researchers attribute this finding to harassment by the mother-in-law.

WHENEVER MY IN-LAWS CAME TO VISIT, they brought my son treats. He began to expect the treats with each visit, which I didn't think was good. So I asked my in-laws not to bring him a treat every time. But then my in-laws went the other way, and they hardly brought anything. I don't know whether that was good or not. Be as direct as you can, although you never can be sure of the outcome!

—HELEN REICH
DUBOIS, PENNSYLVANIA
YEARS WITH IN-LAWS: 45

• • • • • • •

WHENEVER THEY ARE WATCHING THE KIDS, your in-laws are in charge. If they are kind enough to keep the kids for you, you basically have to let them do it their own way.

—DALE JENNINGS
FROSTBURG, MARYLAND
YEARS WITH IN-LAWS: 26

• • • • • • •

MAKE SURE RULES—SUCH AS "no swearing" and "don't give the three-year-old a cookie every time he asks"—do not get thrown out the window just because the in-laws are in town. You've worked too hard to establish good rules in the first place to let them slip for reasons like that.

Must remember this for later.

—DENNIS RUSSO
WOODWORTH, OHIO
YEARS WITH IN-LAWS: 14

IF YOUR IN-LAWS ARE ALWAYS giving the kids candy and gifts, suggest that they sit down and do something creative with the kids instead. I had my mother-in-law filling up coloring books, making Popsicle-stick creations, and gluing cotton balls to paper to make all kinds of pictures. And I know my daughter liked doing that stuff better than getting a bag of candy that I wouldn't let her eat anyway.

—BESSIE SARVER
BAZETTA, OHIO
YEARS WITH IN-LAWS: 3

• • • • • • • • •

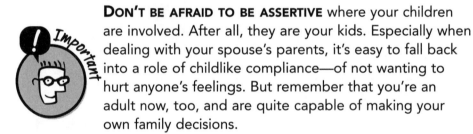

DON'T BE AFRAID TO BE ASSERTIVE where your children are involved. After all, they are your kids. Especially when dealing with your spouse's parents, it's easy to fall back into a role of childlike compliance—of not wanting to hurt anyone's feelings. But remember that you're an adult now, too, and are quite capable of making your own family decisions.

—MARGARET BELTON
PARMA, OHIO
YEARS WITH IN-LAWS: 13

• • • • • • • • •

NEVER, EVER SAY ANYTHING BAD about your in-laws in front of your children (especially young children). Your in-laws will definitely find out about it.

—ANNA ANDERSON
BARLING, ARKANSAS
YEARS WITH IN-LAWS: 48

A BOY NAMED SUE

MY MOTHER-IN-LAW HAS ONE HOBBY: driving me nuts!
This all started the day we came home from the hospital
with our baby boy. As soon as she heard the name we
chose for him, she went crazy. She called us in a panic,
screaming and yelling at us to change the name immediately. She accused us of choosing a girl's name for our
son. She kept saying over and over, "How could you do
this to me? How could you do this to your son? How is
he going to face school, college, with a girl's name?"
She's from another country, where maybe his name *is* a
girl's name, but here it's not. When she realized that she
wasn't going to convince us to rename our son, she had
her relatives call us to change our minds. That didn't
work either; we kept his name. My crazy mother-in-law
didn't even come to see my baby during the first month
of his life because of his name.

—ANONYMOUS
SANTA MONICA, CALIFORNIA
YEARS WITH IN-LAWS: 10

MY MOTHER-IN-LAW WANTS to be called "Nana" by her grandkids. She enforced that rule pretty early, so that's what our kids call her. I didn't really care. My brother-in-law, on the other hand, doesn't comply. His three-year-old calls my mother-in-law (his grandmother) by her first name, and you can see it pisses her off!

—ANONYMOUS
CHICAGO, ILLINOIS
YEARS WITH IN-LAWS: 6

• • • • • • • •

More unexpected visits? I'll have to go under-ground.

UNANNOUNCED VISITS ARE TO BE EXPECTED, and when children arrive, they double. I was expected to stop what I was doing and pay attention. I liked to work in the garden, and my mother-in-law would stop by pretty often. My daughter would yell, "Grandma's here!" and I'd think, well, she'll be entertained for a while. Then after a few minutes she'd yell, "I *said*, Grandma's here." They only visit because they want to see you, so why not do it on your time, when it's best for you?

—C. C.
SEATTLE, WASHINGTON
YEARS WITH IN-LAWS: 28

• • • • • • • •

MY KIDS, MY RULES. If the kid turns out to be a serial killer, it's not my in-laws that society is going to blame for it.

—BILLY TRAMPER
FROSTBURG, MARYLAND
YEARS WITH IN-LAWS: 31

GETTING THE JOB DONE

MY IN-LAWS CAME ALL THE WAY from Nebraska for a weeklong visit with our new baby, their first grandchild. At one point, I was nursing my angel, and I saw a big fat booger in her teeny nostril. A girlfriend was over at the time, and we discussed how I should go about getting it out. She mentioned using a Q-tip, but I had heard that a baby could startle, and the Q-tip might jam right up into the little baby's brain. My mother-in-law, who had been listening to our conversation, offered to hold the baby while we went into the kitchen to get some drinks. Upon our return, there was that big fat booger on the pinky finger of my mother-in-law! I asked how she had retrieved it so quickly. She said, "Well, I just pulled out one of my hairpins and used it to get the thing." Being from the fine state of Nebraska, my mother-in-law still wore a beehive hairdo, which she didn't wash the entire week she was with us. She just sprayed it every day with sticky, chemical hairspray. Up that little nostril went the chemical-covered hairpin. Believe it or not, my baby survived, and even thrived. Learn to laugh!

—SHARI DONNERMEYER
PORTSMOUTH, NEW HAMPSHIRE
YEARS WITH IN-LAWS: 18

A CHILLING EFFECT

WHEN MY HUSBAND'S BROTHER and his wife found out that they were having a baby, they took their families—about 10 people—out to dinner to make the announcement. This news was special because they were announcing the future arrival of the first grandchild for both of their families. However, when they told everyone the news, my mother-in-law shocked us all by saying she was disappointed. She wanted her daughter, her favorite, to be the one to have the first grandchild. "But this one will have to do because there's no turning back now," she said. The table went silent for a minute and then everyone started talking at once. My sister-in-law started crying, her father tried to comfort her by announcing how happy they were about their future grandchild, my father-in-law covered his face with his hands, and my husband and his brother were trying to get my mother-in-law to say something else that would make the situation better. Even the server seemed flustered. Soon after, everyone got up to leave. I think my sister-in-law's parents will forever hold that night against my mother-in-law, which could make for miserable birthdays and graduations in the years to come.

—K.M.
COLUMBUS, OHIO
YEARS WITH IN-LAWS: 1

DON'T GET RILED UP WHEN YOUR IN-LAWS buy your kids gifts that you think are inappropriate. I had to bite my tongue when my father-in-law got things for my son that I didn't want. One gift was a rolling walker. All of my child care books said they were dangerous, and he could reach items that were higher up when he was sitting in it. I hid the walker in the garage.

—CECELIA REEVES
CHICO, CALIFORNIA
YEARS WITH IN-LAWS: 11

· · · · · · · ·

MY MOTHER-IN-LAW COMMENTED harshly on how my husband and I are raising our kids. Even though my sister-in-law tried to talk with her, my mother-in-law refused to admit that she was wrong. We went for months without speaking to her, but finally for the sake of our kids, my husband gave in and called.

—ANONYMOUS
HELLERTOWN, PENNSYLVANIA

· · · · · · · ·

YOU'D THINK SOMEONE WHO raised four kids herself would know not to give kids as much junk as she gives our kids. I'm hesitant to say anything because she's doing us a favor watching them. But she'll give them ice cream and cookies and brownies, all in one sitting. It's just too much.

—M.K.M.
OWINGS, MARYLAND
YEARS WITH IN-LAWS: 1

MY HUSBAND AND I HAVE AN AGREEMENT that we will each deal with annoyances from our own parents and siblings. One year we visited his family in Florida with our six-month-old daughter, who hadn't yet started eating solid foods. My husband's mother and sister tried to feed her everything from bread to cranberry dessert and pushed the issue when we told them no. Because of our previous agreement, I could sit back and let my husband tell them, "You parent your kids and we'll parent ours." Later, when it was my mom who expressed disapproval with the way my husband disciplined our daughter with a "time out," I stepped up and told my mom to butt out.

> *The job's hard enough without criticism from others.*

—ALISA BAUMAN
EMMAUS, PENNSYLVANIA
YEARS WITH IN-LAWS: 7

• • • • • • • • •

IF YOU DON'T WANT TO HAVE KIDS, be patient with your in-laws. Let your new family learn what your reasons are. Share explanations with the extended family. We told people that we enjoyed spending time with children in the family and asked family members not to exclude us from those activities. Show an active interest in nieces and nephews, and then you'll be part of everything. We recently had one niece stay with us while she finished her master's degree. We're very close with the "kids" in the family.

—FRANNE DAVIS
CHAMPAIGN, ILLINOIS
YEARS WITH IN-LAWS: 12

MY MOTHER-IN-LAW HAD THE NERVE to call the other day and say that my four-year-old son was too young to start preschool. I was blown away by this. Not because she is wrong, but because she actually presumed to say such a thing. I understand she's concerned, but you have to let your in-laws know—as I did in this situation—that you will raise your kids as you want. I told her that everyone has the right to an opinion but to keep hers to herself in the future.

—KADESH HARDIE
FROSTBURG, MARYLAND
YEARS WITH IN-LAWS: 4

. . . .

BEFORE I HAD MY FIRST BABY, I spent hours and hours worrying about the impact my in-laws were going to have on him. I think I worried so much because I feared losing control to my mother-in-law. But once my son was born, I never felt like I didn't have control over how he was handled. I realized that my mother-in-law probably butted heads with me because she was the one afraid of losing control. My son is a year and a half old now, and I try to step back and let my mother-in-law interact with him in her way, but I have the satisfaction of knowing that I have ultimate authority over how we raise him.

—ANONYMOUS
EMMAUS, PENNSYLVANIA
YEARS WITH IN-LAWS: 3

DUELING GRANDMAS

DON'T LET THE MOTHERS-IN-LAW take care of the kids together when you are out of town. My mom and my wife's mom shared babysitting duties once when we were on vacation, and though they got along great up until that point, a figurative frost descended while we were gone. We never got a story that matched up completely between mothers, but there was apparently an argument on childrearing styles. I think at the heart of it was two grandmas who get sugar-high on their grandkids and don't like sharing them. These days, it's either one mother-in-law or the other who's in charge of the kids.

—ANONYMOUS
ATLANTA, GEORGIA
YEARS WITH IN-LAWS: 10

• • • • • • • •

IF I GET MY MOTHER-IN-LAW together with my mother, they just talk each other's ears off about the grandkids and leave me out of it, which is great.

—E.F.
HARTFORD, CONNECTICUT
YEARS WITH IN-LAWS: 2

WHEN I WAS IN THE HOSPITAL GIVING birth to my first child, both my parents and my husband's parents stayed at our house. They had both visited before, but never at the same time. When I got home, my house was immaculate, and my husband let on that both his mother and mine had been trying to "out-clean" each other while I was gone! When he suggested that was a great reason to have more kids, I told him that we should simply invite them over more often—but at the same time!

—CAROL R.
PHILADELPHIA, PENNSYLVANIA
YEARS WITH IN-LAWS: 6

• • • • • • • • •

WATCH OUT WHEN TWO GRANDMAS compete to see who can be the most fun! Let me tell you, it's not a pretty sight, although the kids always enjoy it.

—M.A.
SEATTLE, WASHINGTON
YEARS WITH IN-LAWS: 8

MY SISTER-IN-LAW CAME TO HELP us when our twins were five weeks old, and she stayed for two weeks. That was a little tense. She kept wanting to tell me not only how to run the house but how to raise five-week-old twins. Basically, I just lied to her. If she would contradict me, I would just say, "The doctor said to do it this way," and she would say, "Oh, OK." I just kept telling myself that she would be leaving soon.

—ANGELA
WAKE FOREST, NORTH CAROLINA
YEARS WITH IN-LAWS: 8

• • • • • • • •

FOR YEARS, MY MOTHER-IN-LAW acted like she didn't like me one bit. I was nervous about having kids because I thought my relationship with my mother-in-law would get even worse. But the strange thing is, it didn't. Once our first baby was born, my mother-in-law changed. I think that she finally took the time to understand me. And slowly I began to understand why she did the things she did, which made them less painful for me.

—JAN
ALLENTOWN, PENNSYLVANIA
YEARS WITH IN-LAWS: 9

ONE TIME, RIGHT AFTER MY SON WAS BORN, my husband's mom came to visit. As she walked in the door, she started talking about how she had to stop every few miles to throw up because she had a terrible stomach virus. I usually put up with whatever craziness she presented, but this time I made my husband be the bad guy and get her out of the house—without her even seeing our son!

> —ANONYMOUS
> ATLANTA, GEORGIA
> YEARS WITH IN-LAWS: 10

. . . .

ONCE WE HAD KIDS, my relationship with my in-laws really started to deteriorate. This is going to sound silly, but here is what I did: I bought both of them those obnoxious T-shirts that say World's Greatest Grandfather/Grandmother as a gift from the baby. They were absolutely thrilled. They mention—and wear—those shirts all the time, especially around the baby. I'm not saying my relationship with them is now perfect, but it's better.

> —C.J.
> BULGER, PENNSYLVANIA

And this is called T-shirt diplomacy.

MY IN-LAWS TREAT MY HUSBAND LIKE he's five years old when it comes to him taking care of the kids. They are always offering unsolicited advice about how we should deal with discipline, schooling, and so on. When our kids were babies, they'd even tell us how to hold them. All of this was coming from people who didn't even know how to use a car seat! We listen and nod, and then we do whatever we were going to do in the first place.

When in doubt, nod.

—DENISE
CITRUS HEIGHTS, CALIFORNIA
YEARS WITH IN-LAWS: 4

• • • • • • • •

MY MOTHER-IN-LAW WAS ALWAYS on my side when it came to the kids. I don't ever remember her criticizing anything I did with them. When we were coming up with names for our son, my husband hated the name I came up with. But his mom stepped in and said, "She has the right to name the baby because she goes through all the pain of giving birth." So I won.

Check This Out

—NOLA R. SMITH
TAMPA, FLORIDA
YEARS WITH IN-LAWS: 32

All in the Family: Siblings, Aunts, Uncles, Cousins . . .

T he old adage stands: *When you marry a person, you marry their whole family.*

Your mother- and father-in-law are just the tip of the familial iceberg. New aunts and cousins and new siblings-in-law are also part of the equation now and are trying to gauge how you will fit into their cozy, possibly dysfunctional, tree—and you may not.

It is enough of a social experiment to put a group of strangers in a room and ask that they get along. It is a whole other thing to expect to embrace all of those strangers as family.

You rarely hear people discuss their sisters- or brothers-in-law. They do not seem to be as significant in your future life as your partner's parents will be. But that's a mistake.

Show an active interest in your future siblings—you want their vote of confidence, too. Even though it may currently feel as if your mother- and father-in-law are immortal, your siblings-in-law will probably be around longer than their parents. And if you're on their good side, they're more likely to help you when their folks are being difficult on you or your partner.

Finding something you all have in common is a great way to connect. With Michael's siblings, it was the classically cheesy '70s show, "Three's Company." I can spend hours watching episodes with Michael's brother and sister, and laughing together is a great way to bond.

The more I read about other people's sibling problems, the more I am grateful for Michael's brother and sister and my soon-to-be new siblings, Tanya and David.

I REALLY LIKE MY HUSBAND'S BROTHER. The other siblings get highly emotional over issues in the family, but the brother will just throw money at a problem so he can stay uninvolved. I kind of like that about him.

—ANONYMOUS
CHICAGO, ILLINOIS
YEARS WITH IN-LAWS: 6

• • • • • • • •

I'M 5 FOOT 6 INCHES TALL AND WEIGH 115 pounds: most people would say I'm skinny. My sister-in-law, on the other hand, is a fat horse! I don't know how tall she is, but 250 pounds on any frame is overweight. Every single time the family has dinner together, which is at least once a week, she comments on my food intake. If I order two desserts, she'll exclaim, "Look at her; she's double-fisted!" She tells her brother that I'm eating too much. This really bothered me at first, but I eventually learned to ignore it.

> I'd be tempted to slap her with a celery stalk. But patience, patience. . .

—ANONYMOUS
LOS ANGELES, CALIFORNIA
YEARS WITH IN-LAWS: 1

• • • • • • • •

I DON'T MIND GETTING TOGETHER with my wife's family, but when my wife and her sister start fighting like they're in high school again, I begin to wonder why we made the 300-mile drive to her mother's house.

—ANONYMOUS
EMMAUS, PENNSYLVANIA
YEARS WITH IN-LAWS: 6

THE FIRST TIME I MET MY BROTHER-IN-LAW, he was drunk, so the next time we got together I brought him a six-pack of beer: instant buddies.

—STEVEN GREEN
LOS ANGELES, CALIFORNIA
YEARS WITH IN-LAWS: 10

• • • • • • • •

DON'T CONFIDE TOO MUCH IN YOUR in-laws about the problems in your marriage. When my husband and I were going through a tough time, I vented to my sister-in-law. It didn't turn out to be a wise decision. Not only did she repeat it to everyone, but she portrayed me as the bad guy.

—LISA A.
PHILADELPHIA, PENNSYLVANIA
YEARS WITH IN-LAWS: 10

GROUNDS FOR DIVORCE III

In 2006, a British court awarded $65,000 to Gina Satvir Singh, who claimed her mother-in-law kept her a virtual prisoner in their shared home and forced her to perform demeaning chores, such as cleaning the toilet without a brush. Singh, who divorced her husband in 2003, brought suit under the Protection from Harassment Act.

My youngest sister-in-law idolizes my husband and wants to marry somebody just like him. Even though it's kind of sweet, that took some getting used to.

> —Anonymous
> Chicago, Illinois
> Years with in-laws: 6

• • • • • • • •

When my sister-in-law calls my wife, she always calls twice. No matter how long they speak, she calls back five minutes later. My wife doesn't even relax after the first phone call. She knows the second one is coming. We love her sister, and we don't want it to stop, but it's our inside joke. If my wife doesn't have time for two phone calls, she doesn't pick up the phone when she sees it's her sister on caller ID.

> —Anonymous
> Piscataway, New Jersey
> Years with in-laws: 19

• • • • • • • •

I thought my wife's brother was arrogant because he would always talk about his limousine business and would never eat with the family on get-togethers. But when my wife and I visited him on the East Coast, he drove us around in one of his limos, and we didn't want for anything. I changed my mind about him that weekend.

Some people take some time to get to know.

> —Ruben Reeves
> Chicago, Illinois
> Years with in-laws: 10

MY WIFE'S YOUNGER SISTER IS MARRIED to a guy who is biased against Latinos, including Cubans. He thinks they ruined Florida. And yet he married a Latina. My wife and I hate him. We handle it by avoidance, most of the time. But my wife is more blunt than I am. When he says something insulting about Latinos, my wife will say something back to him about the English, but then laugh. But I can tell from her eyes that she's more angry than playful. I'm more diplomatic. I try to get him to talk about computers, because I figure that's relatively safe.

—ANONYMOUS
ATLANTA, GEORGIA
YEARS WITH IN-LAWS: 10

• • • • • • • • •

MY MOTHER-IN-LAW LOVED to spoil her boys. My husband's brother was so spoiled that he routinely ate his dinner on a TV tray while sitting on the couch and watching television; everyone else sat at the table. When we invited him over to our house for dinner, my husband told me to expect his brother to eat in front of the television, but I balked at that idea. I told him that I didn't want his brother setting an example for our two daughters. What would I tell our kids if they asked to eat in front of the television after seeing him do it? When the time came for dinner, I told his brother I wanted him to eat at the table, and he respected my wishes.

—ROSEMARY SUSZYNSKI
NORTH TONAWANDA, NEW YORK
YEARS WITH IN-LAWS: 31

EVENTUALLY, AFTER FOUR CHILDREN, my brother and sister-in-law divorced. If there was a culprit in the divorce, it was my brother. As a result, I felt greater affinity toward my sister-in-law than toward my own brother. The lesson here is that blood is not always thicker than water.

—ANONYMOUS
CHANDLER, ARIZONA
YEARS WITH IN-LAWS: 25

* * * * * * * *

MY BROTHER-IN-LAW WAS ALWAYS trying get-rich-quick schemes. One time he came to visit my parents on their ranch and tried to sell them dirt! Our ranch has 800 acres; what would we do with more dirt?

—SHELLEY BEAUMONT
GRANDVIEW, TEXAS
YEARS WITH IN-LAWS: 4

Note to self: Never buy dirt from an in-law.

* * * * * * * *

MY HUSBAND'S AUNT RAISED HIM and his sister after their parents died. My kids call her Nani (Grandma), but I know her as Aunt Marion. She's an amazing woman. She's 86, and she still has her mind. She curses like a sailor. She's tiny. She's got six children, counting my husband and his sister, and about 32 great-grandchildren. She loves my husband like a son. To her, there's nothing bad you can say about him. I love her to death, mainly because of what she did for my husband.

—ANONYMOUS
NEW CITY, NEW YORK
YEARS WITH IN-LAWS: 29

MONEY, WORK, BUSINESS ... AND YOUR IN-LAWS

DON'T EVER, UNDER ANY CIRCUMSTANCES, get hauled into a conversation with your in-laws about your personal finances. I made the mistake of telling my father-in-law how much money I make a year, and now all I ever hear from him is how I could make more money in other fields.

> —BRITTANY MELLOR
> ZELIENOPLE, PENNSYLVANIA

• • • • • • • •

THINK TWICE ABOUT WORKING with your in-laws in a family business. My mother-in-law is a part-owner of the marina my husband runs. He wants to change things, but she doesn't like change or the money it takes. They argue about it constantly. And it's not just the business issues but the 40 years worth of family stuff, too. When there is a family relationship, it can be hard to insist on change or tell people some of the hard truths you need to in a business relationship. We've come to the point now where we are looking for an exit strategy so that she and Kevin won't work together. That will ease tension.

> —ANDREA COX
> GRAND LAKE, COLORADO
> YEARS WITH IN-LAWS: 13

MY IN-LAWS WERE A CHALLENGE because they were wealthy and liked to use their money to manipulate and control their children and their children's partners. My partner and I agreed that we would not take money from his parents for any reason other than personal gifts at Christmas and on birthdays. I can't say we weren't tempted occasionally when money was tight and his parents would offer to bail us out, but we stuck to our agreement, and as a result, we didn't feel like we had to take their advice about how we should live our lives.

—JOANNE WOLFE
NESKOWIN, OREGON
YEARS WITH IN-LAWS: 8

• • • • • • • •

MY HUSBAND IS THE TYPE who employs our whole family in his business. When his sister's husband lost his job, although he had no experience, my husband put him to work; after all, they had four kids. Eventually, it wasn't working out too well, and my husband had to change him to part time. My sister-in-law saw it as being fired. She turned my husband's parents away from us. At first, I tried to hang on, taking my children to see their grandparents. But it got very bitter. Consequently, my children have grown up without this family, although they live 10 minutes away. It's a shame.

—CAROL
MAHWAH, NEW JERSEY
YEARS WITH IN-LAWS: 25

STICK UP FOR YOUR SIBLINGS-IN-LAW when they're feuding with their parents about something. Take, for example, my sister-in-law's decision to transfer colleges three times in as many years. On the next family phone fiesta or holiday extravaganza, bring up the subject and state very clearly that you think it's a good idea and that your sister-in-law is making the right decision for herself. Switching colleges shows flexibility, adventure, and perhaps a cost savings if moving from a private to a public institution. By backing up the sister-in-law, you show her that taking risks is OK and, even more important, that Mom and Dad are wrong.

You go, girl!

—J.P.
SEATTLE, WASHINGTON
YEARS WITH IN-LAWS: 6

• • • • • • • • •

MY BROTHER-IN-LAW CALLED US from the bus depot and told us the guy who was supposed to pick him up wasn't home, and he wanted to know whether he could hang out at our place until he could get in touch with this guy. We said, "Sure," and three weeks later he was still at our house. I found the best way to deal with my in-laws was to set boundaries and stick to them. You have to say, "Your brother is more than welcome to stay with us for a week." Or, "I don't mind if your mom comes to our house for Christmas dinner every other year."

Check This Out

—CHARLOTTE PARKER
DES MOINES, IOWA
YEARS WITH IN-LAWS: 10

A TALE OF TWO SISTERS

MY SISTER-IN-LAW AND I are like oil and water. I've come to refer the time we spend together as "the battle of the bitches." We never seem to be on the same page. For example, we visited her once for a week at the beach. I'm very budget-conscious, and she doesn't understand the concept. At the end of our week, my cash was low and she suggested that we go out to dinner. I told her that my husband and I had only $20 left to spend for the both of us to eat. "I know just the place," she said. As soon as we walked in to the fancy, New York–style restaurant, I knew our $20 wouldn't make it through a proper meal. We ordered as little as possible, while she and her boyfriend ordered appetizers, steaks, and drinks that added up to about $60. When the meal was finished, she actually turned to us and asked, "Do you want to split the bill?" The answer was a loud "no!" We won't go out to dinner with my husband's sister unless we have cash to burn.

—A.F.
EMMAUS, PENNSYLVANIA
YEARS WITH IN-LAWS: 4

SOMEONE'S GOT TO BE FIRST

MY SISTER-IN-LAW IS THE QUEEN of one-upmanship. Whatever you can do, she can do so much better. If you say you run six miles a day, she can run 12. If you just read a great book, she just read the best book ever. If you have a master's in psychology, she has a doctorate in psychiatry. If you had a root canal, she had both wisdom teeth pulled. It got to a point where there was competition about who had our name first because we have the same full name through marriage. It became this sneering, snarling exchange. She said, "So who had the last name first?" because she married into it before I did. I'm a few years older, so I said, "So who had the first name first?" It makes my hair stand on end that I have to share my name with this person who rubs me the wrong way all the way down the line. I can't kill her, and I can't force her not show up at family functions, so I have to grit my teeth. I just keep my distance and wave from far across the room.

—BONNIE
FLORAL PARK, NEW YORK
YEARS WITH IN-LAWS: 36

A FRIEND OF MY EX-HUSBAND'S FAMILY once called me to tell me that my husband's sister was constantly saying negative things about me. When I confronted my husband about the issue, he looked at me as if I was crazy and said, "Let's call her and figure this out." When we called, my husband remained silent while I confronted her. She went crazy and accused me of being selfish and not caring about his family. Then she hung up on me. My husband never said a word. This conversation sealed the separation deal.

—ANONYMOUS
LOS ANGELES, CALIFORNIA
YEARS WITH IN-LAWS: 1

ONE OF MY BROTHERS-IN-LAW WAS into bodybuilding in his early 20s. He eventually got involved in the restaurant business, which took a lot of time, so he gave up the bodybuilding. In his house, though, he had built a gym, complete with leg machines, a treadmill, racks, mirrors, a television, music—it was set up like a real gym. It sat dormant for about 15 years. As he and I got closer, we started lifting weights there. We're on our fifth year of lifting together. I go to his house Monday, Wednesday, and Friday mornings at 5:30 a.m. We've become so close he just bought a new restaurant and I lent him the money, without a contract.

That's what I call getting to know your in-law's strengths!

—ANONYMOUS
PISCATAWAY, NEW JERSEY
YEARS WITH IN-LAWS: 19

WIFE PLUS

MY FATHER-IN-LAW REALLY EXPECTED us to fill traditional gender roles. I was expected to do all the domestic work, have a job, and raise the kids to perfection. My husband was expected to have a well-paying job and be the boss. I don't cook, but I do pay bills. I make most of the rules and do discipline; he brings home the money. Things balance out and we're fine with the way things work. At least my mother-in-law knows us well enough now as a couple, and she respects the way we do things.

—MELISSA
MUNCIE, INDIANA

• • • • • • • • •

MY HUSBAND WAS LEAVING for work one morning and my mother-in-law, who was visiting, said to me in horror, "You're sending him out wrinkled!" I was surprised that she expected me to be responsible for his appearance, like I was his mother. I said in a calm, factual tone, "He knows how to iron. I don't do that." Don't take your in-laws' expectations personally. You don't have to feel bad or guilty or defend how you do things. It's not about you; it's about them. If you can, address it directly, without anger. Otherwise, let it go in one ear and out the other.

—ANONYMOUS
EASTON, PENNSYLVANIA
YEARS WITH IN-LAWS: 20

I GOT MY FIRST HINT OF my mother-in-law's expectations of me during my first visit to my husband's parents' house. My fiancé sat down in their recliner and told his mother he was hungry. She asked him what he wanted to eat, listing everything she had in the house that she could make for him. Then she waited on him hand and foot, making the meal, putting salt and pepper on it, and serving it to him in the recliner. I looked right at her and said, "There is absolutely no way I would have done that for him." Her expression communicated her disapproval.

—ANONYMOUS
WILLIAMSPORT, PENNSYLVANIA
YEARS WITH IN-LAWS: 8

· · · · · · · ·

I WAS EXPECTED TO TAKE OVER all social and familial contact with my husband's parents and their friends; holiday gifts, thank-you notes, planning visits, making phone calls. I just didn't do it. I told my husband, "I'll take care of my family, you take care of yours." I'm sure I was considered a very bad daughter-in-law.

—MARIA
BROOKLYN, NEW YORK
YEARS WITH IN LAWS: 26

FOR SEVERAL YEARS, MY HUSBAND and I had my sister-in-law over for dinner on Thanksgiving. Every year, I would get up early to roast the turkey, peel the potatoes, fix the stuffing, and do the hundred other things that go into preparing a Thanksgiving meal for a family. But inevitably the day would end with me watching my hard work walk out the door: My sister-in-law would come over empty-handed, feast with the rest of us, and sit around while I cleaned up. Then, just as she was getting ready to leave, she'd announce that she would take the leftovers home with her, and—no lie—she would pack up everything that was left and walk out the door.

—ROSEMARY SUSZYNSKI
NORTH TONAWANDA, NEW YORK
YEARS WITH IN-LAWS: 31

• • • • • • • •

MY HUSBAND HAS A MEDDLING sister who is old enough to be his mom, so she acts like his mom—and my mom, too. It's hard because she's the oldest in her family and I'm the oldest in my family, and we're both used to getting our way. Just remember that your interactions with your in-laws are brief. You make your own family, and you set your own rules. When you visit with your in-laws, just take everything with a grain of salt, and remember that after you leave, you're going back to the life you want.

—ANGELA
WAKE FOREST, NORTH CAROLINA
YEARS WITH IN-LAWS: 8

HUSBAND PLUS

AFTER MY FATHER DIED, my mother expected my husband to be at her beck and call. My father used to do everything she requested within minutes. She would usually call my husband late, because she slept all day and stayed up all night. It would be 10 p.m. and she'd call him up and say, "You have to come over and put the screens in the windows." He would already be in bed, and he'd get up and go. One time the phone woke me up at midnight and I thought, "Oh my god! I hope she's all right." And she said, "Something's wrong with my television clicker." I said, "Mom, he's sleeping. Get out of your chair and turn on the television." But she insisted that he come over immediately and fix it. And he got up and went! It turned out that the batteries were dead. Even though my husband knew my mother could be a demanding pain in the neck, he loved her. It's true that the way a man treats his mother—or mother-in-law—says a lot about how he'll treat other women.

—LINDA
PORT JEFFERSON, NEW YORK
YEARS WITH IN-LAWS: 30

MY HUSBAND'S SISTER AND I were friends before I met him. Over time, unfortunately, she has become more and more like his mom. I'm not friends with her anymore, and he's not close to her, but she has followed us to three states, and each time she moves in right by us. We're moving again, but we're not telling her ahead of time, and this time we're going to figure out how to keep her from following us.

—HANNAH
HOUSTON, TEXAS
YEARS WITH IN-LAWS: 11

* * * * * * * *

MY BROTHER-IN-LAW IS A FOUL-MOUTHED cretin who loves being a bachelor and telling me about his weekend escapades with women. I used to just nod my head in the right places hoping he would go away. One day it dawned on me what to do. He started talking in graphic detail about a girl he had bedded the night before, and I told him if he didn't stop, I'd tell him where his sister's birthmark was.

—JIM
PITTSBURGH, PA

Check This Out!

There's a true sibling relationship.

* * * * * * * *

MY BROTHER-IN-LAW BEGGED for money all the time, not a lot, but $10 here and $20 there. So I just made him work for it. After a while, he didn't need money anymore.

—RUBEN REEVES
CHICAGO, ILLINOIS
YEARS WITH IN-LAWS: 10

SIBLING DYNAMICS

I knew my brother-in-law for a few years before I got to know Michael. David was this funny guy my sister worked with. I looked forward to saying hello to him every time I stopped by their office. When his brother and I started to date, I thought it could only get better. My sister and David were good friends; we could all be amazing siblings. It sounded so perfect.

I soon discovered that dynamics change in a group of people when one relationship changes. Our siblings were not thrilled when we started to date, and each warned their respective sibling about the other's commitment issues.

I have no doubt that they were protecting us, but they also admitted later that they were worried about what this meant for their own friendship. If Michael and I had a messy break-up, how would it affect our siblings? That never even crossed my mind. A year later, things are back on track and we are all finding a new way to be a friendly family. My sister and future brother-in-law are now excited when they see each other at family functions, and David even said that my relationship with his brother has provided endless entertainment when he gets together with my sister—apparently they do a dead-on imitation of the two of us. It just goes to show that siblings never really change.

I'll pass this one on to Michael. No joke.

DO NOT JOKE ABOUT ATTRACTIVE women with your brothers-in-law or father-in-law, not unless you are really good friends. They might be guys like you, but they are still protective of their sisters. One time I made some off-hand remark about a girl walking by, and my brother-in-law did not take it well.

—MARK DELVECCHIO
PHILADELPHIA, PENNSYLVANIA
YEARS WITH IN-LAWS: 14

• • • • • • • •

MY HUSBAND WARNED ME ABOUT HIS SISTER. He told me that if we gave her an inch, she'd take a mile. He warned me repeatedly, for example, not to say, "Stay as long as you'd like," because she would stay for weeks, months, or indefinitely. At first, I thought he was exaggerating. But sure enough, after our son's birthday party, when she said how delicious the cake had been, I told her to take some leftover cake home. So she took the whole cake, and left us none!

—K.C.
SAN FRANCISCO, CALIFORNIA
YEARS WITH IN-LAWS: 4

Trouble-in-Law: Dealing with Difficulties

It seems as if every family has one member whom people suspect of harboring a secret. Some relatives may know what it is (some may only pretend they do), but no one talks about it. There are other relatives who seem like characters on a TV sitcom: the wild one, the weirdo, the impossible one, the oddball. But no sitcom script could duplicate my own experience with family secrets.

One day, when I was a child, I flipped on the TV and there on The Donahue Show was my great uncle's wife, Elizabeth (also known as "The Contessa"). She was sitting on the guest chair and Phil

Donahue asked her, "What is it like to be the oldest Madame in North America?" That was how I learned about that branch of the family's business.

I asked Michael what skeletons hang in his family closet and he replied, "You want me to let out the skeletons? I say, let sleeping dogs lie! My family is perfect—don't think of them any other way."

Every family has a few secrets; some entertaining, and some devastating. It is important to keep your perspective and ask yourself, "How much does this really affect me?" It is also important to respect the fact that each person is entitled to some privacy. Not every family fact is meant to be public knowledge or broadcast on television.

DON'T COUNT ON YOUR IN-LAWS to act the same way that your parents act. In fact, don't even count on your in-laws to act the same way that their child (your future spouse) acts. I had expectations based on how my parents handle things and based on my husband's personality, and I was all wrong: my in-laws are nothing like my parents.

> —DENISE
> CITRUS HEIGHTS, CALIFORNIA
> YEARS WITH IN-LAWS: 12

· · · · · · · · ·

THE HARDEST THING FOR ME has been learning how to set boundaries. My wife and her mother are really close, but to me her mother is a little—what's the word?—stifling. For instance, if we have dinner with them, it's an all-day thing. And even though Sunday is our only day off together, her mother can't see why we wouldn't want to spend every Sunday with them. If we say we can't come, it's like, "What do you mean you can't come this week?" They just don't understand why we wouldn't want to be with them as much as possible. So it's been a matter of setting boundaries, telling them we can't stay all day.

> —JASON T.
> CHAPEL HILL, NORTH CAROLINA
> YEARS WITH IN-LAWS: 5

THE FIRST TWO YEARS MY WIFE AND I were together, my father-in-law drove me nuts. The four of us would get together often, and my father-in-law would always make some statement during the evening that made me see red. One night he said, "You know, Hitler had some good ideas." That set me off, and an hour later we were still debating the pros and cons of the Nazis. This happened many times, and every time, my wife and mother-in-law would become strangely silent and either start reading or just leave the room. One night, after another heated debate, my wife said, "Why do you take the bait? He only does it to get a rise out of you!" After a few embarrassing seconds, I started laughing. It was his way of testing me and finding out the true character of his son-in-law.

I hate tests. What if I flunk?

—SCOTT A. MOORE
EISLEBEN, GERMANY
YEARS WITH IN-LAWS: **17**

BLOWING OFF STEAM

When you've just got to vent, go online. There are a number of forums on the Web dedicated to hearing and, perhaps, helping with in-law trouble; among them:

     www.tortureddaughterinlaws.com
     www.ihatemyinlaws.com
     www.love.ivillage.com/fnf/fnfin-laws

I WORE MY IN-LAWS DOWN with my charm and humor. I refused to be insulted by their reticence or occasional snide comments; it was just a test. I laughed things off and didn't take things personally. When my in-laws were in a car accident a few years ago, my partner and I sat up all night with them in the hospital. My father-in-law was a standoffish fellow; when I hugged him, it was like hugging a stick. But after the accident, he told me, "You have been so good to my wife and me," and he had tears in his eyes. After that, it wasn't like we were best buds or anything, but he acknowledged that I wasn't going anywhere and that I knew what true partnership meant.

I've always believed in killing with kindness!

> —V.M.
> DENVER, COLORADO

• • • • • • • •

DON'T GO LOOKING FOR A HALLMARK relationship with someone else's family, or have some fairy-tale fantasy of how it's going to be, and you won't be let down. I'd hoped I could have a more normal, stable, fun relationship with my husband's family than I'd had with my own. When I realized that wasn't going to happen, I was very angry and disappointed.

> —ANONYMOUS
> SAN DIEGO, CALIFORNIA
> YEARS WITH IN-LAWS: 15

> *Note to self: Get a hotel guide for my own city.*

THE FIRST TIME I PUT MY FOOT DOWN was when we lived in a tiny, tiny apartment. My in-laws not only showed up on our doorstep to spend their vacation with us, but they brought my mother-in-law's sister and her sister's friend! We had no warning at all. A couple of us shared the bed, and others were on the sofa, the floor, everywhere. I left and stayed at a friend's house. Later I apologized—big mistake! When you know you're right, don't ever backtrack just to make peace.

—HANNAH
HOUSTON, TEXAS
YEARS WITH IN-LAWS: 11

* * * * * * * *

I LEARNED NOT TO RELY ON MY IN-LAWS for anything, and never to ask them for anything, because it will give my mother-in-law the power to say no, which she relishes. The upside is that every time they give us something, it's a pleasant surprise.

—ANONYMOUS
YEARS WITH IN-LAWS: 5

* * * * * * * *

Consider

I ALWAYS MAKE SURE to have the wine ready when my mother-in-law comes to visit. That way, she can have a drink immediately and mellow. It drastically reduces her need to tell me what to do.

—ELIZABETH
FORT WAYNE, INDIANA
YEARS WITH IN-LAWS: 7

ALL THAT GLITTERS

MY WIFE AND I HAD BEEN LIVING in our house about two months, and we had bought the furniture for the dining room and the living room, but we were going slow on decorative stuff because we wanted to look around. We went on a trip to Aruba for a week. When we got home and turned on the lights, we were hit with the glitter and reflections of ultramodern mirror-and-glass etched pictures in the living room and the dining room. It was like walking into a prism! The few things that we had put up were gone. There were giant nail holes everywhere, and the pictures were hung unevenly. Everything was completely out of line with our style. I put everything into boxes and brought it back to my mother-in-law's house. I handed her the stuff and said, "Here are some gifts that I'm sure you'll like." Things were pretty hot for a few weeks after that, and the incident was always thrown in my face whenever we had words. My wife wouldn't say anything to her mother because she didn't want to upset her.

—GENE WILLIAMS JR.
SEAFORD, NEW YORK
YEARS WITH IN-LAWS: 15

BEFORE I COULD KNOW MY IN-LAWS WELL, my husband was diagnosed with melanoma. We were very young and had been married only a few months. My in-laws seemed to be in denial. They told me I was exaggerating the situation, questioned my methods of care, told me I was giving up, and accused me of having secret cash. After he died, I stopped speaking to them for more than two years. Back then, I felt like everything they were doing was directed at me. Now I know that it wasn't about me; it was about the death that none of us could bear but had to handle in our own way.

—KATHRYN
LONG BEACH, CALIFORNIA
YEARS WITH IN-LAWS: 2

• • • • • • • •

I HAD A CONFRONTATION with my mother-in-law in which I made her cry. My husband and I were in her kitchen arguing about whether or not he should go to a junkyard to buy car parts he didn't need. Obviously, I was the one who didn't want him to go, but his mother interrupted me and told me, "He can go." I told her the conversation was between my husband and I and that she should stay out of it. When she started crying, I thought maybe I should have been a little softer in the way I conveyed my message.

—ANONYMOUS
WILLIAMSPORT, PENNSYLVANIA
YEARS WITH IN-LAWS: 8

Consider

IT'S ALL RELATIVE

The more people I interview, the more I realize that every family (really, everybody) is off its collective rocker. Behavior I deem normal—for example, when we fly together, we all hold hands while the airplane takes off—probably seems a little odd from my fiancé's point of view. He loves them, but I'm more concerned with him liking them. What does he appreciate and what drives him a little nuts? I know that "normal" is probably just what we're used to. So I asked Michael what little insignificant oddities he had noticed about my family. Here's what he said:

"Your mom has to vacuum-seal each item of food before she gives me a doggie bag to take home. The food is fresher two weeks later than when she made it! She should be a spokesperson for shrink-wrap.

"Your father has to get the latest technology two months before it comes on the market. I worry that he may be part of some kind of technology mafia.

"Your parents like the best of everything, but they are not uptight. I really love spending time with them. Your mother is warm, charming, very caring, and a fantastic cook (which makes me hang out there more often). Your father has an abundance of knowledge and if I need an expert opinion, I know where to go.

"I am more comfortable with them than with past girl-friend's folks. They are the nicest in-laws I have had (this is my first marriage)."

Sounds perfectly normal to me.

MY IN-LAWS ARE SO . . .

. . . bitter that their son married me. Nothing I could ever do would be good enough for them. I think even if I won the Nobel Peace Prize I wouldn't be good enough. But I stopped trying to please them a while ago. You have to be who you are and find happiness in your own heart.

—A.P.
CORRIGANVILLE, MARYLAND
YEARS WITH IN-LAWS: 3

* * * * * * * *

. . . rich. And I can't think of any other adjective that would describe my in-laws. The better part of it is that they aren't stingy with the money. They like to throw it around to their kids. And I love being able to be there to catch it.

—G.M.
CUMBERLAND, MARYLAND
YEARS WITH IN-LAWS: 28

* * * * * * * *

. . . happy together. They're great role models for my own marriage. I know I'm lucky.

—PATRICK
NEW YORK, NEW YORK
YEARS WITH IN-LAWS: 10

MY MOTHER-IN-LAW DOESN'T LIKE ME. She's sent me flaming e-mails and said hateful things to me and about me—things that are untrue, like that I'm responsible for the death of her husband. I've stopped taking it personally: It's not about me, but about her. I never bad-mouth her to my husband or my child. I make sure she knows that she is always welcome in my home. She doesn't come, but if she did, I would treat her with respect. But I don't go there. If my husband wants to see his family, he goes there. I see no reason to subject myself to the stress that being on her turf would generate.

Yikes!

—R.J.
REDMOND, WASHINGTON

• • • • • • • •

NEVER COMPLAIN TO YOUR MOTHER-IN-LAW about your husband. The second time my in-laws came to visit, my mother-in-law commented about how neat and tidy our house was. Annoyed, I replied, "The only reason our house is clean is because I follow your son around and pick up after him." Completely serious, she replied back, "Your job is to keep your house nice for your husband." I was ready to scream, but instead I bit my tongue, smiled, and let it slide. This really works: my mother-in-law and I have a great relationship today.

—PAMELA BARTH
BAKERSFIELD, CALIFORNIA
YEARS WITH IN-LAWS: 25

WHEN MY HUSBAND AND I FIGHT, neither of us calls our parents and complains, "So-and-so did this to me!" They're parents: After you and your spouse make up, and everything is all lovey-dovey, they'll still harbor a grudge because they think someone hurt their baby.

—VANESSA HAIRSTON
HIGHLANDS RANCH, COLORADO
YEARS WITH IN-LAWS: 5

• • • • • • • •

KEEP TALKING TO YOUR SPOUSE about how you feel about your in-laws. It's not going to happen overnight, but someday he'll understand. Many times when we would arrive at his parents' house, his dad would say "Hi" to my husband and ignore me and the kids. Before one visit, I told my husband exactly what was going to happen, and he finally saw it.

—W.F.
MERTZTOWN, PENNSYLVANIA
YEARS WITH IN-LAWS: 22

> *Having a sense of humor has certainly saved me many times.*

• • • • • • • •

I'VE LEARNED TO SUCK IT UP, embrace the differences, find the good in everything you can, and laugh as much as possible. I've also learned that if I feel strongly about something, I need to speak up when appropriate and discuss the matter with others. Life is just too short to do anything else.

—ANONYMOUS
DALLAS, TEXAS
YEARS WITH IN-LAWS: 20

STAY INSIDE THE CIRCLE

WHEN MY WIFE AND I WERE FIRST MARRIED, we didn't really separate from our own families, as the experts say. Our counselor explained that we each had "one foot in our marriage and the other foot with our families." She explained that a family is like a circle, and when you marry, you create an entirely new circle that includes only your spouse and eventually your children. Your spouse must have your complete loyalty and trust, after all. This is the person you will grow old with. If you betray that by confiding to your mother, brother, aunt, and so on about things involving your spouse, you've gone "out of the circle." Once you're married, your loyalties have to shift from your parents to your spouse. The most important person in your life is the one you're married to!

—CRAIG
BETHLEHEM, PENNSYLVANIA
YEARS WITH IN-LAWS: 9

A PEEK AHEAD

I did not anticipate that my introduction to a number of Michael's relatives would occur at a funeral. When his aunt died after a long illness, I had to decide if I was close enough to the family to attend the service. I realized that my presence there was a sign of my respect for Michael's family, but mourning is a very personal process, and I was not sure how I would be received.

I wasn't too surprised that I felt comfortable being there: what amazed me was that during the service, a number of relatives comforted *me*. A few of them put their arms around me and asked me if I was OK. What a family. The last thing I'd expected from them, at such a time, was that they would worry about an outsider.

And I *was* comforted, as a matter of fact, because I realized that this was the kind of family that would gather together to help one another in times of trouble. If I needed help in the future, I could count on them.

WHEN I FIRST MADE MY HUSBAND stand up to his mother for me, I wanted to know everything that was said: what he said, what she said. After a while, though, you see that he's showing respect for your relationship and thinking of you, and I don't ask him every detail anymore.

—HANNAH
HOUSTON, TEXAS
YEARS WITH IN-LAWS: 11

. . . .

OF ALL THE WOMEN I DATED IN MY LIFE, the only parents I didn't get along with were the parents of the woman I married. Her mother and I butted heads on everything, to the point that, a month before our wedding, my mother-in-law-to-be was still trying to set her daughter up with someone else. But she came around.

True love triumphs again!

—B.B.
PORTLAND, OREGON

. . . .

TRY TO UNDERSTAND what it is about you that enables your mother-in-law to drive you crazy. It's not a relationship you can change, so you're better off looking at yourself and figuring out what it is about you that allows her to push your buttons. I realized, for example, that I was secretly afraid I would turn into my mother-in-law. Once I realized I wasn't going to, she didn't drive me as crazy anymore.

—SARAH
MINNEAPOLIS, MINNESOTA

SKELETONS IN THE CLOSET

ON MY THIRD DATE WITH MY FORMER WIFE, she invited
me to go to a baptism with her family. The reception hall
was very overdone, with gold and red velvet wallpaper
and an ornate brass Venus de Milo oil lamp. Once we
were seated, the waiter arrived with an ice bucket and a
bottle of Dom Pérignon for her father. Everyone else had
Ripple wine with screw caps. I said to my wife, "What is
that? How come he gets what he wants?" And she said it
was because her mother likes Dom Pérignon. Then,
before dessert, some guy went over to her father, got on
his knee, and kissed his hand! I grabbed my wife and
said, "Why is he kissing your father's hand? I thought
your dad was in industrial kitchen design." She started
crying and told me that he's in the Mafia, I shouldn't ask
any questions; the less I knew, the better. I was bothered
and embarrassed by the secret, but also really intrigued.
We tried to live our lives independent of this reality, but
when my son was born, we became yoked in and
exposed to it once again, and that wasn't acceptable to
me. Still, I believe that as long as you're part of a family,
you're obligated to keep to yourself any skeletons you
find in the closet, so that's what I did.

—ANONYMOUS
SMITHTOWN, NEW YORK
YEARS WITH IN-LAWS: 20

MY WIFE started talking about this guy who was trying to come over from another country to the United States, and he was asking her parents for help. He was asking her parents for help was because he was my wife's father's son—my wife's half-brother by another woman. He was a little bit older than my wife, but not much. Her father used to be quite the ladies' man. I stayed out of it: Since my in-laws speak another language, there are times when it can be useful to have a language barrier. I just pretended I didn't know what they were saying.

—ANONYMOUS
ATLANTA, GEORGIA
YEARS WITH IN-LAWS: 10

• • • • • • • •

THREE DAYS BEFORE MY WEDDING, my father-in-law went missing. We finally found him in jail. He had been arrested for soliciting an undercover police officer. I found out from my wife's cousin that my in-laws had not had sex in 25 years. I've been married for three so far and I'm praying that this doesn't run in the family. So far so good!

—ANONYMOUS
LOS ANGELES, CALIFORNIA
YEARS WITH IN-LAWS: 6

Consider

THE IN-LAWS' CONFIDENCE in you strengthens over the years when they see that above all else, you love and support your spouse. Petty annoyances tend to fall away.

—C.C.
SEATTLE, WASHINGTON
YEARS WITH IN-LAWS: 28

· · · · · · · ·

MY FATHER-IN-LAW WAS NEGATIVE from the get-go. My husband told him that I was a singer and actor. My father-in-law's comment was that he hated music, never liked it. He said that all musicians and singers are just trying to get money out of people for performing. He went on to say that actors are just liars. He was a produce manager, so I said, "Tell you what: You won't buy my records and I won't buy your fruit and we'll both be just fine." That ended his comments about the arts, and he has not bothered me about it since.

—ANONYMOUS
BIRMINGHAM, ALABAMA
YEARS WITH IN-LAWS: 4

Perhaps all of us need a 'Mantra Manual' when dealing with in-laws.

· · · · · · · ·

YOUR IN-LAWS ARE HUMAN BEINGS, TOO. They have feelings and needs. Each time they overstep a boundary, take a deep breath and chant your mantra: "They're not *my* parents. It's all going to be OK." Repeat three times.

—ANONYMOUS
SAN FRANCISCO, CALIFORNIA

I HAVE LEARNED TO BE LESS DEFENSIVE around my in-laws. What sometimes may appear to be a judgmental statement can actually turn out to be good advice. I just had to let down my wall of pride.

> —RACHELLE
> BEGGS, OKLAHOMA

They are not my parents. It's all going to be OK.' (Mantras do work well!)

. . . .

KILL YOUR MOTHER-IN-LAW WITH KINDNESS: It works like a charm. And remember, behind closed doors, you don't have to take any of her advice!

> —JENNIFER
> DALLAS, TEXAS

. . . .

TO ME, MEDDLING IS ANY ACTION by the in-laws that was not initiated by you. If you need to ask them for help or for their input on something, that is fine. But any time they take it on themselves to inject their opinion—or worse, their actions—on some aspect of your married life, they have crossed the line. I'll admit that I have turned to my in-laws for help over the years; we all need help from time to time. But there have also been occasions when they have done things like buy coats for my kids because they felt the old coats were too worn. I know they just want to help, but it can be insulting.

> —RAY VINCET
> LAVALE, MARYLAND
> YEARS WITH IN-LAWS: 15

MENTAL CASES

THERE SHOULD BE A SUPPORT GROUP for people and their in-laws. You just can't prepare yourself for this new relationship. These people treat you like a child, like they're your parents, and it doesn't fit. These people have an opinion about you and how you should do things, and you're like, "Who are you? I have my own parents for that!"

—ANONYMOUS
TORONTO, CANADA
YEARS WITH IN-LAWS: 3

• • • • • • • • •

YES, I DO HAVE THE WORLD'S worst mother-in-law. This woman has been married and divorced four times and does not believe in happy relationships. She mentally batters everyone who marries one of her children. I have tried everything, including going to a therapist, to understand why she is so awful. The therapist said that she is a crazy beast and should be avoided. My husband knows that his mother is nuts, too, and has agreed that we only have to see her four days a year. I would prefer no contact at all, but he feels sorry for her.

—CARLA HIGGINS
OAKLAND, CALIFORNIA
YEARS WITH IN-LAWS: 8

IF YOUR BOYFRIEND OR GIRLFRIEND SAYS, "My family is crazy," believe them! When my boyfriend told me his family was crazy, I thought, "I know them; they seem all right." I told him, "Oh, everybody says that." But, no! His family *is* crazy.

—HANNAH
HOUSTON, TEXAS
YEARS WITH IN-LAWS: 11

• • • • • • • • •

HANGING OUT WITH THE IN-LAWS, you're probably under stress and you don't even know it. I used to have a stomach problem; I got over it, but every time I'd visit my wife's family for dinner, it would flare up as soon as I sat down at the table, and I'd have to excuse myself. Apparently I was stressed, even though I didn't feel nervous. But my stomach would just freak out, and that would be it for the night.

—S.H.
ATLANTA, GEORGIA
YEARS WITH IN-LAWS: 10

NAGGING IS ONE OF THE WORST THINGS an in-law can do, because it makes you feel stupid. If they're so worried about your situation, they should sit down and help you develop a concrete plan. When we were starting out, me, my wife, and our three girls lived in a rental house in the ghetto because it was all we could afford. Never once did my mother-in-law offer to lend us money, help us develop a budget, or assist me in finding a better job. Instead, in an extremely judgmental voice, she kept telling us to move out of that house immediately.

—LENNARD HAYNES SR.
HOUSTON, TEXAS
YEARS WITH IN-LAWS: 4

• • • • • • • •

EARLY IN MY MARRIAGE, my mother-in-law tried to do too much. She was bringing us food, giving her daughter money, offering to decorate our house. It may be that your in-laws are just trying to be helpful. So, handle it tactfully. I said, "I know you love your daughter very much. I appreciate your doing everything. But that may hurt my marriage in the long run." I also said, "We need to figure some things out on our own. If we stumble, we'd like to be able to come to you for advice." She understood.

—THOMAS M.W. "MIKE" DOWNS
FAYETTEVILLE, NEW YORK
YEARS WITH IN-LAWS: 18

MY MOTHER-IN-LAW HAD THIS CRAZY HABIT of coming to our home and rearranging the knickknacks on this little shelf we have over the home entertainment center. At first I thought she was doing it to get a rise out of me, but when I asked her one day, she said she was just arranging the pieces in a more logical fashion. Every time she left I would change them back. It was really upsetting to me until I decided to just leave them the way she had them. I think it was more upsetting to her when I wasn't playing into her hands.

Rearranging things? I'd go nuts.

—MARTIN SEABECK
FOMBELL, PENNSYLVANIA

• • • • • • • •

MY IN-LAWS HAVE HAD TROUBLE LETTING GO. My 35-year-old sister-in-law still has to ask her mom's permission if she has to miss the family's weekly dinner. Last year, someone had offered her tickets to a film-festival event and she had to call and ask if it was OK. Her mom said no, so she declined the tickets. I was shocked that a 35-year-old woman had to ask her mommy's permission. My husband had no idea when we first met how messed up things were. He thought my parents were weird for being so laid back, but he soon realized he felt more comfortable and more himself around them. My husband loves his parents, but he doesn't like them.

Amazing!

—ANONYMOUS
TORONTO, CANADA
YEARS WITH IN-LAWS: 3

MY MOTHER-IN-LAW IS A LOVELY LADY, but totally over-bearing. She'll buy me stuff for the house from out of state, mail it to me, then call me up and argue with me over the phone about where it goes. I've learned just to nod and smile during our conversations, then rant and rave after we hang up. I avoid a lot of conflict this way.

—ELIZABETH
FORT WAYNE, INDIANA
YEARS WITH IN-LAWS: 7

· · · · · · · · ·

MY MOTHER-IN-LAW is one of those people who blurts out whatever she thinks. When we were first married, I bought a dress that I was excited about, and I took it out to show her. She said, "I'm sure it must have looked better on you than it does on the hanger." I was stunned. From that point on, I didn't share too much.

—LESLIE
FARMINGTON HILLS, MICHIGAN

· · · · · · · · ·

DON'T FEEL BAD IF YOU occasionally wish your mother-in-law were dead.

—SARAH
MINNEAPOLIS, MINNESOTA

· · · · · · · · ·

BITE YOUR TONGUE until there are holes in it!

—ANONYMOUS
SHELTON, CONNECTICUT

MY MOTHER-IN-LAW IS VERY INSECURE, so she tries to control every situation she's in. She puts people down loudly, then laughs like it's just a harmless joke, but it is so off-color and mean-spirited that she just makes people feel uncomfortable. She's trying to subtly make everyone understand that she has the upper hand, but she just shows her own pathetic side.

That's not funny . . .

—ANONYMOUS
YEARS WITH IN-LAWS: 5

• • • • • • • •

JUST ACCEPT IT: PEOPLE ARE DIFFERENT. And in-laws are often the most different people that you'll ever meet. My mother-in-law was a nice person, but she and I had nothing in common. When I had an article published in a prestigious magazine, she just said that I was a good mother and that was enough for any woman. I understood then that she would never understand my ambition beyond my family. We began to get along better because I did not try to force her to understand me, nor did she try to force me to be like her. We just accepted our differences.

—NANCY NEIBERG KOSANOVICH
NAGS HEAD, NORTH CAROLINA
YEARS WITH IN-LAWS: 37

IN-LAW TROUBLE TIPS

I can see that what I've learned in my training as a life coach can be applied to relationships with my in-laws. Here's how I'd approach in-law trouble from the point of view of a life coach.

- **BE PRESENT.** It is easy to get caught up in stories of how your in-laws were overbearing while you were planning the wedding, or how your father-in-law criticized your job on one of your first meetings. While these things can certainly shape a relationship, it is important to judge your in-laws by how they treat you *now*. Looking back, you may have wished you had done something different in dealing with them.

- **LOOK AT THE PICTURE FROM DIFFERENT ANGLES.** What you see as negative may be appreciated by someone else in the same situation. The way you see something makes a difference. You may look at your father-in-law as overbearing instead of overly caring. You may find that your mother-in-law's habit of cleaning up your house is actually a great thing. Ask yourself: How do I currently view my in-laws? What would a good relationship with my in-laws look like? What do I want? Design your life from this vantage point, instead of being a passive participant in the relationship.

- **APPRECIATE THAT WE ALL HAVE DIFFERENT VALUES.** This will help create more understanding. Friction often exists between people because each one is expressing a deeply important value. What you do for a living does not always reflect who you are, so try not to judge your in-laws from this place. To figure out your values versus those of your in-laws, think about how each of you would choose to spend a vacation, your favorite topics of conversation, and what each person's hobbies are. You will get a sense of a person's values by listing these things.

Then imagine that it is a year from now and this issue is resolved and you are very content. What did you do to make that a reality? What changes did you have to make in order to change the situation?"

I'd tell him to keep the change!

THE MOST INSULTING THING that happened to me was when my father-in-law offered to get me a job where he worked. He told me that it was backbreaking, hard labor, but that it paid about $1.50 more an hour than I was making in a job I liked. I looked at him like he was from another planet. Then I told him, "Thanks, but no thanks."

—BARRY FITTERER
CUMBERLAND, MARYLAND
YEARS WITH IN-LAWS: 17

More Wisdom: Good Stuff That Doesn't Fit Anywhere Else

Here's an example of good timing: Editing this book gave me a window into in-law situations and relationships just when I most need to know about them. True, the book also gave me some new things to worry about, but even so, I'm grateful for the knowledge. Some say ignorance is bliss, but I believe that it is important to enter the in-law relationship with your eyes open.

I also believe that many things in life are about expectations. While it is helpful to hope for the best in many situations and to have faith, it is also important to keep in mind that adjusting to a new family takes time and patience. You can love your in-laws and still hate some of their quirks. Hold onto your sense of perspective. When you are feeling most frustrated, it may help to know that hundreds of people in this book and out in your community are your allies.

So, what does the future hold for me and my new family? I have the unfair and perhaps creepy advantage of being able to ask my father-in-law this question through more coffee-cup conversations.

Will we be successful? Will our families grow closer? How many grandchildren will Michael and I give him? I hope he does not see eight or nine little ones swirling around in his cup. I hope he sees joyful family gatherings and respectful but lively exchanges, and that the positive feelings our families now have only grow deeper and stronger.

I'll drink to that.

TAKE A MULTIFACETED APPROACH: 1) Smile a lot when around them, 2) pretend you don't know them, and/or 3) remind yourself it could be worse: They could be *your* parents.

> *I'll take choice #1!*

—K.K.
FALMOUTH, MAINE
YEARS WITH IN-LAWS: 35

• • • • • • • •

PRETEND TO BE INTERESTED when they are telling stories about people you don't know. It can be horribly boring at times, but it is important to them, so just grin and bear it.

—SUE
SEATTLE, WASHINGTON

• • • • • • • •

FIGURE OUT WHAT YOU CAN LIVE with and what you're going to push back on. That's the best way to handle tricky in-laws.

—ANONYMOUS
CHICAGO, ILLINOIS
YEARS WITH IN-LAWS: 6

• • • • • • • •

DON'T GET INTO A DRINKING MATCH with your father-in-law. No matter how chummy he may be with you at the time he suggests or implies it, it's better to avoid any sort of situation where you can't control the outcome.

Consider

—B.A.S.
FREMONT, CALIFORNIA

ASK FOR HELP, EVEN IN SOME SMALL WAY. It makes your in-laws feel needed. I would call and ask them to clip grocery coupons for me. Then, when I went grocery shopping, I would drop my child off at their house and pick up the coupons. Also, remember, the phone rings both ways. I would write on a chalkboard in the kitchen, "Call the P's." That would remind me to be in touch. In-laws need love, too!

—JANE DEBATTY
DENVER, COLORADO
YEARS WITH IN-LAWS: 17

I love this advice!

• • • • • • • •

TREAT YOUR SPOUSE WELL. That's the best gift you can give your in-laws.

—JESSE
CASTRO VALLEY, CALIFORNIA
YEARS WITH IN-LAWS: 1

• • • • • • • •

AFTER 15 YEARS OF MARRIAGE, my in-laws and I get along well. It all feels simple now, but it used to be stressful. My sister-in-law just got married and is suffering. I told her that she has to believe that her mother-in-law is trying to act in her best interest. I've told her to put her emotions on the back burner and to be direct. One way to be direct is to gently say to your in-law(s), "It troubles me when you do X," or "It helps when you do Y."

—CINDY
SEATTLE, WASHINGTON
YEARS WITH IN-LAWS: 15

PLAY THE NAME GAME: The words *mother-in-law* and *father-in-law* have such negative connotations in our society that I make a conscious effort not to think of my in-laws that way. Instead, I think of them as "Michael's mom" or "Michael's dad." It's just semantics, but it feels so much more positive, and it works for me.

Works for me...

—JENNIFER BRIGHT REICH
HELLERTOWN, PENNSYLVANIA
YEARS WITH IN-LAWS: 2

* * * * * * * *

BOTH OF OUR FAMILIES WERE OPPOSED to my wife and I getting married because we were still students (with no way to support ourselves) and we came from different religious backgrounds. We decided to run away and get married at a friend's house in the Middle East. After the ceremony, we flew to London and stayed there a full year. We told our parents in letters. During that time, they calmed down. By the time we moved back to Chicago, everybody came to the airport to greet us, and they were happy. This taught me that, within your relationship, you need to make the decisions. You should let the in-laws know what these decisions are and they can choose to take part in them or not. But you can't live your life to please them.

—EMILIO E.
VANCOUVER, B.C., CANADA
YEARS WITH IN-LAWS: 33

THE BEST WAY TO GIVE IN-LAWS unexpected news is to give it to them straight, put a positive spin on it, rehearse the key sentence, and try to find out beforehand if they secretly hate you. Also, do it on their turf—it gives them more confidence, and you can leave if it really goes pear-shaped.

—A.M.
CAMBRIDGE, MASSACHUSETTS
YEARS WITH IN-LAWS: 1

. . . .

WHEN YOUR IN-LAWS ARE TALKING and you've had enough of it, sometimes you have to do the same thing you do when you're tired of your kids: Just let them talk. It doesn't really matter if you're listening or not; if they think you are, they'll stay happy!

—RUTH
BURLINGAME, CALIFORNIA
YEARS WITH IN-LAWS: 25

. . . .

PAY ATTENTION TO WHAT YOUR IN-LAWS SAY; they've known your spouse a whole lot longer than you have. Before my wife and I got married, my father-in-law remarked, "Has she started slamming doors yet?" Apparently, she liked to slam doors when she was angry. She hadn't done it yet, but just a few short months later ... *slam!*

—ANONYMOUS
ALLENTOWN, PENNSYLVANIA

KEEP YOUR SENSE OF HUMOR, and don't take anything personally. One day, my husband and I visited our in-laws and had an evening of intense talk about buying a house, children, and other such topics. The conversation eventually turned to actors, and someone mentioned Robert De Niro. My mother-in-law declared: "I don't like that man. I have a hard time looking at him with that mole on his face. It's going to become cancerous and kill him." Well, I have an almost identical mole on my face. An awkward silence followed as she realized her faux pas. I've never seen my husband so embarrassed, but I just had to laugh, remembering all the times I've put my foot in my mouth.

> —N.B.
> LOS ANGELES, CALIFORNIA
> YEARS WITH IN-LAWS: 1

DON'T GET TRAPPED IN A WHITE LIE; it can haunt you. My husband took me up to meet his folks, and his mother had made a gooseberry pie. I hated gooseberries, but I ate that pie. And I made the mistake of saying, "That was the best gooseberry pie I have ever eaten." She was a dear thing, very sweet. Every time we drove up to see them from that point on, she made a different dessert for everyone else, but gooseberry pie for me.

> —F.
> RAYMORE, MISSOURI

YOU MAY NEVER BE ABLE TO CHANGE your mother-in-law's controlling behavior, but you can change the way you deal with it. You can do that by laughing about it with friends, quietly continuing to do things your own way, or reacting with humor instead of impatience when she starts to dictate the best way to carve a turkey.

—TIM LAKE
BADEN, PENNSYLVANIA
YEARS WITH IN-LAWS: 22

Note to self: Buy phone card.

• • • • • • • •

CALL YOUR MOTHER-IN-LAW. Frequently.

—JENIFER MANN
CASTRO VALLEY, CALIFORNIA
YEARS WITH IN-LAWS: 1

• • • • • • • •

LONG AFTER I HAD BEEN DIVORCED from her son, my mother-in-law from my first marriage came down and babysat my kids for 10 days while I went to Europe with my new husband. I had never been to Europe before, and she was thrilled that I was getting the chance to go. The day we left, I was dressed in this really nice outfit and hat, and when she saw me, she started crying. She said, "Oh, you look so beautiful." She wasn't an in-law; she was like a mother to me.

—NOLA R. SMITH
TAMPA, FLORIDA
YEARS WITH IN-LAWS: 32

MAKE YOUR IN-LAWS YOUR FRIENDS. Try to show some interest in what they are about. Establish a good relationship and create some memories with them—one on one, and not only with other family members.

—N.S.
CHICAGO, ILLINOIS
YEARS WITH IN-LAWS: 30

• • • • • • • •

I'M NOT MUCH OF A BEER DRINKER, I don't much like football or baseball, and I don't smoke—those manly bonding activities. My wife's dad is a "manly man": He smokes cigars and drinks whiskey and talks about baseball and makes crude jokes about women and sex. I love him dearly, but it's hard to find a lot of common ground. He has a different view of what it means to be a man. But I try to show an interest in the things he cares about. I'm not a baseball fan, for instance, but when my in-laws came to visit last summer, I took my father-in-law to a baseball game. And I'm not dishonest about it. He knows I'm not a fan, but that I just wanted to take him. During the game, he was chatting me up about the strategies of the game, and without being dishonest, I showed an interest. I asked him questions and took the opportunity to learn something about baseball. I knew I would never be as passionate about it as he is. But that doesn't mean I couldn't try to understand him.

Attitude is everything.

—ANONYMOUS
ATLANTA, GEORGIA
YEARS WITH IN-LAWS: 10

IF YOUR SPOUSE SAYS SOMETHING bad about his parents, don't agree with him. It's OK for him to vent about his parents, but it's not the same if you do it. Once, when my husband and I came back from a weekend with my mother-in-law, I was thinking that she was so stressful to be around; she didn't sit still the entire weekend. To my surprise, my husband said the very same thing out loud. But when I agreed with him, he got mad!

—ANONYMOUS
ALBURTIS, PENNSYLVANIA
YEARS WITH IN-LAWS: 7

> *And I feel blessed to have such loving guides.*

• • • • • • • • •

BOTH MY MOTHER-IN-LAW AND FATHER-IN-LAW are lovely, and I can't do without them. I think good in-laws are partners in life with you. They precede you and they act as good guides if you want them to be. It's good to ask them what they would do over, if they had the chance.

—FRANNE DAVIS
CHAMPAIGN, ILLINOIS
YEARS WITH IN-LAWS: 12

• • • • • • • • •

UNLIKE MANY PEOPLE, I actually get along with my mother-in-law really well. In fact, I talk to her more than my husband does. Our phone conversations last so long that I had to buy two telephone headsets—one for me and one for her!

—DEBBIE
SAN ANTONIO, TEXAS
YEARS WITH IN-LAWS: 33

I LOVE MY MOTHER-IN-LAW. She's very genuine and self-sacrificing. She'll do anything to protect the kids. She's 85 and always tells people to "leave Lucy alone!" (that's her). We get together often, and she vents to me. I could choose to see that as a burden, but I actually really like that she feels comfortable enough with me to release the pent-up stuff. When she sits with me, it all comes out. I let her be who she is; she didn't get that response from the rest of her family.

> —E.P.
> MILFORD, CONNECTICUT
> YEARS WITH IN-LAWS: 5

. . . .

DON'T TRY TO CHANGE your in-laws; you can't.

> —ANONYMOUS
> CHICAGO, ILLINOIS
> YEARS WITH IN-LAWS: 6

. . . .

PEOPLE LIKE SOMEONE who is a good sport. Every family knows they are crazy in their own way, and if you are willing to participate in the craziness, they'll cut you a lot of slack, no matter how bad you are at darts.

> —ANONYMOUS
> BOSTON, MASSACHUSETTS

SPECIAL THANKS

Thanks to our intrepid "headhunters" for going out to find so many respondents from around the country with interesting advice to share:

Jamie Allen, Chief Headhunter

Andrea Fine	Jennifer Bright	Natasha
Andrea Syrtash	Reich	Lambropoulos
Barton Biggs	Jennifer Byrne	Pete Ramirez
Besha Rodell	Jenny McNeill-Brown	Ralph Fox
Gloria Averbuch	Joanne Wolfe	Robin Lofton
Heather Leonard	Kazz Regelman	Sally Burns
Helen Bond	Ken McCarthy	Shannon Hurd
Jade Walker	Linda Lincoln	Staci Siegel
Jennifer Batog	Lisa Hubbell	
Jennifer Blaise	Lorraine Calvacca	
Kramer	Marie Suszynski	

Thanks, too, to our editorial advisor Anne Kostick. And thanks to our assistant, Miri Greidi, for her yeoman's work at keeping us all organized. The real credit for this book, of course, goes to all the people whose experiences and collective wisdom make up this guide. There are too many of you to thank individually, but you know who you are.

CREDITS

Page 16:   http://people.emich.edu/jboynton/research/aust-
           ralian.html
Page 30:   *The Independent* (London), March 15, 2006
Page 70:   *New York Times*, March 15, 2003
Page 104: www.ananova.com
Page 148: *The Economist*, October 17, 2002
Page 166: *Little India*, September 4, 2006

HOW TO SURVIVE THE REAL WORLD

"Stories, tips, and advice from hundreds of college grads who found out what it takes to survive in the real world."

—Wendy Zang
Knight Ridder/Tribune News Service

"Perfect gift for the newly minted college graduates on your list."

—Fran Hawk
The Post and Courier (Charleston, SC)

HOW TO SURVIVE DATING

"Rated one of the Top 10 Dating Books."

—About.com

"Invaluable advice ... If I had read this book before I made my movie, it would have been only *10 Dates*."

—Myles Berkowitz, Filmmaker
Wrote, Directed and Went Out on *20 Dates* for Fox Searchlight

"Great, varied advice, in capsule form, from the people who should know—those who've dated and lived to tell the tale."

—Salon.com

HOW TO SURVIVE YOUR FRESHMAN YEAR

"This book proves that all of us are smarter than one of us."

—JOHN KATZMAN
FOUNDER AND CEO, PRINCETON REVIEW

"Voted in the Top 40 Young Adults Nonfiction books."

—PENNSYLVANIA SCHOOL LIBRARIANS ASSOCIATION

"This cool new book ... helps new college students get a head start on having a great time and making the most of this new and exciting experience."

—COLLEGE OUTLOOK

HOW TO SURVIVE YOUR TEENAGER

"Parents of teens and parents of kids approaching those years will find wisdom on each page ... provides insight, humor, and empathy ..."

—FOREWORD MAGAZINE

"With warmth, humor and 'I've been there' compassion, editors Gluck and Rosenfeld have turned the ordinary experiences and struggles of parents into bits of compact wisdom that are easy to pick up and use straightaway. I especially liked this book's many examples of how to survive (and even thrive) while living under the same roof as your teen."

—JACLYNN MORRIS, M.ED.
CO-AUTHOR OF I'M RIGHT. YOU'RE WRONG. NOW WHAT?
AND FROM ME TO YOU

HOW TO SURVIVE YOUR BABY'S FIRST YEAR

"What to read when you're reading the other baby books. The perfect companion for your first-year baby experience."

—SUSAN REINGOLD, M.A.
EDUCATOR

"How to Survive Your Baby's First Year ... offers tried-and-true methods of baby care and plenty of insight to the most fretted about parenting topics ..."

—BOOKVIEWS

"Full of real-life ideas and tips. If you love superb resource books for being the best parent you can be, you'll love How to Survive Your Baby's First Year."

—ERIN BROWN CONROY, M.A.
AUTHOR, COLUMNIST, MOTHER OF TWELVE, AND CREATOR OF
TOTALLYFITMOM.COM

HOW TO SURVIVE GETTING INTO COLLEGE

"... chock-full of honest, heartfelt, and often funny advice from not just experts but the folks who have been there and done that—college students and their parents ... the book covers everything college students are bound to confront. Topics are covered with a can-do attitude that helps take the fear factor out of what often is one of the most stress-inducing projects families tackle together. As with anything else in life, it helps to talk to people who've done what you're planning to do. This book compiles the experience of hundreds of students and parents who have survived getting into college."

—JENNIFER BURKLOW,
CHICAGO SUN-TIMES, OCT. 10,2006

HOW TO LOSE 9,000 LBS. (OR LESS)

"Informative and entertaining … a must-read if you have ever struggled with the delicate 'D' word."

—Zora Andrich
Reality Show Contestant

"Something here may get you through a hard patch or help you lose those final few pounds."

—Jim Kiest
San Antonio Express-News

BE THE CHANGE!

"This is a book that could change your life. Read the stories of people who reached out to help somebody else and discovered they were their own ultimate beneficiary. It's almost magic and it could happen to everyone. Go!"

—Jim Lehrer
Executive Editor and Anchor, NewsHour with Jim Lehrer

"An inspiring look at the profound power of the individual to make a positive difference in the lives of others. *Be The Change!* Is more than an eloquent tribute to volunteer service—it increases awareness of our shared humanity."

—Roxanne Spillett,
President, Boys & Girls Clubs of America

"Civic involvement is an enriching joy, as the people in this book make clear. It's also what makes America so great. *Be The Change!* provides practical advice and awesome tales that could change your life. This is a wonderful and inspiring book."

—Walter Isaacson,
CEO, Aspen Institute

HERE'S WHAT THE CRITICS ARE SAYING

"The next 'Dummies' or 'Chicken Soup'… offers funny but blunt advice from thousands across America who've walked some of life's rougher roads."

—DEMOCRAT AND CHRONICLE (ROCHESTER, NEW YORK)

"Colorful bits of advice … So simple, so entertaining, so should have been my million-dollar idea."

—THE COURIER-JOURNAL (LOUISVILLE, KENTUCKY)

"The books have struck a nerve. 'Freshman Year' was the number-one-selling college life guide of 2004 …"

—CNN.COM

ABOUT THE EDITOR

ANDREA SYRTASH was born in Toronto, but has been living in the United States for almost a decade. She received her undergraduate degree at one of Canada's oldest schools, Queen's University, and her postgraduate degree, with honors, in Broadcast Journalism from Ryerson Polytechnic University in Toronto. A graduate of the Coaches Training Institute, Syrtash has been working with clients as a life coach since 2002. She has also written and lectured extensively on dating and living your best life. Most recently, Syrtash co-wrote and hosted a men's lifestyle show on dating for OnNetworks. She has offered advice in various media outlets across the country, including KCBS in San Francisco, *USA Today*, and on NBC's *Today* show, and served as special editor for *How to Survive the Real World*, published by Hundreds of Heads Books.

Syrtash lives in New York City with her fiancé, Michael. *How to Survive Your In-Laws* is one of her favorite Hundreds of Heads titles, since she is currently navigating through this pivotal relationship. She looks forward to using some of the advice in this book through the years with her new in-laws.